Authentic Love

Suzanne Mcgregor

iUniverse, Inc.
Bloomington

iUniverse books may be ordered through booksellers or by contacting:

iUniverse
1663 Liberty Drive
Bloomington, IN 47403
www.iuniverse.com
1-800-Authors (1-800-288-4677)

ISBN: 978-1-4502-9262-7 (sc)
ISBN: 978-1-4502-9263-4 (ebook)

Printed in the United States of America

iUniverse rev. date: 04/27/2012

Contents

True Love	1
Love	2
I Will Let Down My Hair	3
I'm Waiting	4
I Am Alone Without You	5
I Love Your Body	7
As We Romantically Danced	8
Last Night	9
Between the Sheets	10
This Love Is True	11
Turn off the Lights	12
Love Filled	13
Exactly How I Feel	14
I Will Keep My Love Inside	16
Let Me Take Care of You	17
You Can Find True Love	18
I Wanted You First	19
Hard to Say No	20
Sex	21
Midnight Romance	22
I am sure	23
Men & Love	24
Learning to Love	25
Women Are Special	26
Please Touch Me	28
Romancing	29
Expressing My Passion	30
Whenever I Look at You	31
When the Heart Cries	32
Love Pain in the Morning	33
Come If You Love Me	34

We Will Make It 35

Your Spirit Spoke To Me 36

When the Love Dust Settles 37

Your Eyes Tell All 39

The Highest Value Reside Me 40

What I Am Feeling Now 41

Me 43

Allow Me 44

Invisible Love 45

The Bliss 46

A Wonderful Man 47

Dinner for Two 48

It Takes Two 49

I Need You 51

Tough Love 53

Trust Your Decision 55

Tell Me Why 57

Love Me for Who I Am 58

Your Love Is Enough 60

Unique Qualities in You 61

You Left Too Soon 62

I'm Excited about You 64

Let Him Be 65

Unknown Love 67

Sweetness 69

Don't Hide from Me 70

I Love You Inside Out 71

We Have Each Other 72

I Enjoy a Strong Woman 73

Smooth Woman 74

Please Commit 75

I Feel Secure with You 76

I Love a Strong Man 77

You Know I Love You 78

Settling Down with Me   79

Please Stay   80

Beloved   81

Let's Make Up Baby   82

Secret Thoughts   84

I Am Here for You   85

You Are My Left Hand   86

A Strong Relationship   87

My Soul Loves Me   88

The Man I Married   90

I'm Free in This Relationship   92

Give Her Space   93

What I Am Really Thinking   94

I Love Having You Around   95

What Every Woman Wants   97

Chance   98

Why Look for Acceptance   99

What Is He Really Thinking?   101

I Want the Keys to Your Heart   102

It's Hard to Win His Soul   103

Choosing the Voice   104

I Still See Your Face   105

I am Thinking about You   106

You Will Regret   107

Love Will Forgive   109

I Love You   110

Morals vs. Ego   111

Tonight   113

This Love Will Last   114

When We Met   115

Our Love Is The Strongest   117

You're Here Now   118

When the Soul Speaks   119

I Want a Life with You   121

Come Back   122

Listen to What's Inside   124

Nothing Standing in Our Way   126

I Would Not Tell a Soul   127

I Will Marry Him   129

I Believe   130

Holding You   131

Love Without Fear   132

What's Authentic?   133

When My Soul Pulls   134

Sweet Spirit   135

Love Stood in the Rain   137

Bitter/Sweet Love   138

Your Love Changed Me   139

Beautiful Woman   140

Whenever I looked at You   141

I Miss You Tonight   143

I Fell in Love by the Pool   144

A Talk over a Bottle of Wine   145

The Heart Never Lies   147

Love Is Sweet   148

Alone without You   150

In Love with Him   151

Your Love Keeps Me   153

The Love in Your Eyes   155

Here We Are Again   156

I Will Be Patient With You   157

Please Let Me In   158

Let's Try One More Time   159

Take a Risk with Me   160

So Beautiful Tonight   161

Love Was Knocking   162

The Bigger Picture   163

My First Shot at Love   164

Just Relax My Love   165

Relationship + Work   166

You Are Coming   167

I Love a Strong Man   168

You Are Free to Achieve   169

I Love You So Much   170

I Know What I Did   171

I Will Work for Your Love   172

I Admire You   173

Lovers & Friends   174

Listen to Your Heart   175

Let's Disagree to Agree   176

I Thirst for Your Love   177

This Love Is Not Over   178

Let Me Show You Love   179

A Second Chance at Love   180

I am Secretly in Love with You   182

Communication Is the Key   184

You've Been Sweet   185

Spend Some Time with Me   186

Love Stood with Us   187

Love Delayed Not Denied   188

Love is a Language   189

Unleash Your Love   190

I Will Not Hurt You   191

We Belong Together   192

Love Caught Me by the Heart   193

Just Trust   194

Enough Love   195

Let's Settle This First   196

Better Love Life   197

When Our Bodies Call   199

I Fell In loveOver the Phone   200

No One but Us   201

Love Lives 202

The Impact 203

Love Soothes Anger 204

Talk 205

I am Waiting for Your Love 206

Your Soul Knows 207

Your Love Makes Me Weak 208

Love Will Find a Way 209

The Love & Faith Test 210

I Need to See You 212

Let Me Love You 213

Where Are You 214

Make Love to Me 215

I Love You a Million 217

To the Good Life 218

When Love Feels 219

Love Has No Gender 220

Love Will Stand Up 221

Love Knows When 223

Love Can Be Rough 224

Passion 225

Let Love Awaken You 226

So Much Love for You 227

A New Love Is Born 228

Where Is My Love 229

Making Love 230

Just Believe 231

You Will Love 232

Follow the Next Step 233

Love Will Return 234

I'm Confident about Love 235

You Finally Came 236

You Will Commit 237

Let's Talk 238

I Love You The Most   239

I know we belonged.   240

The Love That Flows   241

What's Keeping Us Apart   243

Pain with Love   245

Give Him Space   246

Let's Start Again   248

Please Believe In Me   249

Late-Night Shower   250

Thinking Deeper   251

About the Author   252

True Love

True love genuinely cares
when loved ones are unable to bear!
True love doesn't carry any fear.
True love is confident and will be there;
never revealing the doubt in its heart.
True love will keep you from drifting apart!

True love is constantly thinking how to be true,
trying its utmost best never to offend you!
Always thinking ahead, planning a day to get wed!
Never putting pressure on the soul!
Freezing time so you don't look old …

True love is always thinking of ways to make a joyful day,
Removing all hazards that cause delay!
Looking forward to a blissful day to be born,
keeping every promised that was announced the day before,

Thinking of each other's feelings constantly,
saying sorry even when it was not necessary!
True love is carried out daily—
True love is not used conveniently,
is something that happens naturally

True love appreciates your presence each day,
even in those times when the pressure tries to stay!
Real love will wait until you come home,
It will never let you be alone!

Love

Love understands without anyone having to explain;
love steps back and monitors the entire game!
love knows when you are broke,
even when you are all dressed up in that million-dollar coat!

Love sees the embarrassment on your face
but stands in place, giving mercy and grace!
love warms the bed up when things get cold,
love understands the battle in the streets
and is always armed, ready and will defeat.

Love will fight to keep a roof over our heads,
alerting every one of the possibility that's widespread!
Love will not judge even when in doubt;
It will work over time to prevent a drought

Love will give all that it has without
thinking about what's in the other person's hands.
Love never measures what's being given
but appreciates the thought that comes along with what's hidden.

Love will stand up tall with hands out in case you fall.
Love understands that times will get rough
and is prepared if the other half is not tough!

Love knows that perfections don't exist
and accepts their lovers mistakes with a kiss!
Love is not afraid to speak up when things go wrong
but will speak only when time is allows!

Secrets are freely placed on the floor
to be resolve before anyone hits the door!
Confusion will not loiter on the ground,
because true love will not tolerate it for long!

I Will Let Down My Hair

Tonight I will let down my hair
and enrobe a sexy Red Lingerie
for the one who continues to keep me safe and warm
and senses when a new day is born.
I will happily follow that bliss;
giving him that magic kiss
so the next day he could miss!

My soul will be enrich and complete
in the bedroom under those silky sheets!
I will tell the clock, "Don't stay conscious
Just leave all the timing up to my subconscious

A new direction has settled in my mind;
I will concentrate on enjoying my quality time!
As I venture into his world,
I already feel like an innocent girl,
so soft and full of cheer; when his lips wet me there.

When morning comes he will dance; wondering
where the hell he put his pants!
This feeling will surely appeal me
thinking about how much he pleased me!

As my heart reminiscence how he liberated me
Wondering how soon he will come back to make me tea
I will always remember to let down my hair
And enrobe my sexy red lingerie's.

I'm Waiting

I have gone astray in love over you,
tossing and turning; my heart threaten to be through.
As I wait for you to change your mood
Please let go! So I can soothe

I want to make love to your soul
a burning desire that never goes cold
As I wait for us to journey to that desired place
I will stare at the wine glass sitting to be taste

Tonight you will never forget,
the love making; I will leave no room for regrets
The closer we get the more confident I feel
This love is a signed seal deal!

Men come and men will go,
but you my love makes my adrenaline flow.
I'm aroused by the sound of your voice.
This strong desire is simply my choice.

I will sleep with the lights on just in case you reveal yourself late
so when I open my eyes, you would not have to wait.
I will keep the bed warm so we can comfortably mate,
As I unleash my love in its purest state.

I Am Alone Without You

I am alone without you; my world is so noisy sometime
I am unable to hear you!
When you are close the journey feels right,
so painless not even a fight
When you are near I feel like the world
is sitting at my door; cant helped to be ignored
My life is complete only the rough edges that needs to be neat!

When you are here; my troubles are afraid to come;
they know that you possess a sharp shooters gun!
I see them coming my way; but they just pass on their merry way
Your present is like a consuming flame
The ones that don't belong is expose to shame

I am happy to see misery go to waste;
it plagues when they don't see your face
Your presence is very important to me;
even fear knows it; and trembles at your feet
I get excited when you arrive knowing;
we are heading for the everlasting sky
That's the place I long to be;
Its where I would feel the most relief!

I love you not because of how you look
but because of your exceptional wisdom "oh my" I am hook!
You never complain about the man, who just died
but you see the importance of why he said good-bye!
Your face never sits on the floor;
you are cheerful; it's hard to ignore
Always lifting your expectation for a better day;
waiting and expecting things to be structured a different way!
You always move quickly on your task
You are an original; you know how to make a relationship last!

When I am with you, I hear the universe loud and clear,
It's like drums pounding in my ear!
The message is lucid and without fear
So perfect every trouble can hear
I want more and more of you every day;
I wish I could clip your wings so can stay!

I Love Your Body

You look so appealing grooming your hair.
I am in awe that you took the time to care.
It's really stimulating; beyond compare
how masculine you look in your cute underwear.

You have so much sex appeal
I'm secretly thinking how to get you to reveal
Suppose I change into something see threw
I know you would probably forget about that previous move

This should work to get you to be late?
I will use my provocative self as bait.
No talking; I'll just change into that something.
No questions asked, I will just nakedly passing.

I will lock the door and start to dance
exotically across from where you stand
Smiling as your resistance drew near.
A gentle touch will remove that work fear.

Your masculinity is too hard to resist.
My femininity agreed as I persist.
Thinking you might be late because of me
The good news is; your face will be full of glee!

As We Romantically Danced

Tonight as we romantically danced,
my entire body went into a trance.
As you held me so gracefully
My inside felt cheerfully

As my chest pressed against yours,
the energy invoked my pores.
Then when our cheeks met,
my body whispered; you have not seen nothing yet

Too shy to let me know,
but you searched me out to find my flow!
I wanted to remain guarded for the night,
but our spirit was in sync as we unite

I was prepared to let myself go
and pretend tomorrow would never know.
I will do my best to hide in the dark,
but I know my voice would surely leave a mark.

Dancing so close made it hard to resist
when your sexy gentleness continued to insist.
The night whispered, I should persist
It's an opportunity; I should not miss!

Last Night

Last night I got engaged.
I was so worried about my age.
I am still in awe; it finally came to pass
I know this time the marriage will last

This man has always been so humble and sweet
His quietness was uncertain, but it made me weak
Many times I just wanted to leave.
Then he would say two words and I would believe

Back and forth over time
I just watched him; silently, in my mind,
I often wonder if I leave; would I find
A devoted man that would be more than kind

Like a cat, I patiently wait
in the corner, where he couldn't see my face
I was certain I would see a sign
Letting me know it was time
No sign, but I never risk what was truly mine!

Between the Sheets

Between those silky sheets of mine,
I want to be one with him inside
as his warm lips moved my legs apart,
he gently treaded down my path.
I remembered entering an unknown place
each time he whispered softly my name.

As I slowly closed my eyes,
absorbing his delicious romance
inside where he was safe and warm.
He was more than welcome to stay all night long.

His energy was so strong
pleasing me; I felt I belonged
As he moved up and down, caressing my soul
He was so aggressive and bold

Flowing with pleasure,
playing in my treasure,
I will not use time to measure.
I am so glad I explored this handsome bachelor.

This Love Is True

I knew this love was true
because you sat me down and
explained your point of view
you told me I was your first choice
I heard the genuine substance your voice
Your words was smooth and completely moist

To think about life without you
is like walking the streets naked without shoes.
I feel like I have found the missing piece
To fit in my heart where I keep all my beliefs

I will cherish you until we get to the other side
and still it will be a long way from saying good-bye.
There is almost no stress with you.
Our love sheltered us through as we grew

It's good to pretend that time doesn't exist
So life for a moment can be less complex.

Turn off the Lights

Turn off the lights; let me romance you
I am ready to transcend from this awkward mood
Let me unleash that secure feeling.
Allow me to restore you with some sexual healing

We have been apart long enough
No disturbance; baby it's just us
Open; so I can to tease between your knees.
I love it! When you continuously say please!

Scream with a voice of passion
move your waistline in that romantic fashion.
I love those sweet words you whisper in my ear,
telling me that your orgasm is near
Let's come together and aim for the sky
It's okay; no need to be shy!

Love Filled

As I sit still; I feel so love filled— you are so precious.
I am never sexually, emotionally bored with you
I admire your strength our relationship has sufficient length

I feel so comfortable sharing the same bed;
Where I enjoy cuddling and laying my head
Oh! This feeling is so right
my soul never wants to say good night.

I'm equipped for you and me.
enough love for us to breadth
Seeing you gives me instant relief.
You shield me from a world full of grief.

I enjoy watching movies with you.
It doesn't have to be something new.
I'm just happy in your presence.
You are sweeter than that unknown fragrance

Soft and sweet; you are my treat.
Fixed in my heart so neat
Let's promise to meet after we die.
I have already consulted the creator that sits on the most high.

Exactly How I Feel

I was happy when darkness came
so I could feel like I was being reborn again.
I think I allowed myself in too deep;
climbing was difficult—so steep!

You hold the key to my soul.
Your negative actions took such a toll.
How hurt I was when you left,
how my mind was in mental distress.

Late at night I shivered; so cold,
all my members wanted to let go!
I quickly found the mirror so it could look at me,
and asked myself? What is it I'm supposed to be?

This must have been a show?
I often wondered if he waited for time to ripe to go.
Today I will look for my eyes
and place them back in my head as the rise.

My story will be told.
I will stay young and sweet,
and with all this stress,
I will never grow old!

I felt many times I did not exist,
but reluctantly continued to persist!
Even though I had to endure the waiting list

I wish I could turn the clock around;
I would run faster before I enter that stupid re- bound!
It's no secret how much I loved him.
And how badly our problems needed in a trim
Oh well! Rome was not built in a day,
and it takes more than one man to make it stay

When things got rough, you did not trust.
Without any clothes, you chased the next bus.
Farewell until we meet again
I was tired anyway of playing pretend!

I Will Keep My Love Inside

My love is too precious to run wild outside
without any clothes; I would die!
My heart was placed in your hands,
but you bailed during the course of our plans

The pain was so strong with flame,
In that moment I desperately
needed something to make me sane.
I wanted to uplift my soul—
anything that would take me out of this world!

A sign to lure me through the sky,
the right way showing
me where to go and die!
Many nights I cry
As the pain wanted to stained my inside

Love told my heart that in every good there is pain,
and in one bad experience there can be many gains.
I will keep love safe and sound
in a deep place where it cannot be easily found,

A place where love can call home,
free to romance, and rome
A secret place where love can teach
how to avoid situations that will calls for an immediate breach

Let Me Take Care of You

I'm unhappy without you.
I feel pain looking at things that belong to you.
In the morning when the birds starts to sing,
I think about the fun times we spent last spring!

In the morning when your first leg wanted to touch the floor,
I remember holding you; rubbing you just a little more.
I enjoyed serving you that cup of hot tea,
Along with kissing your back under the sheets

I kept our relationship lily white
I never left it in the dark to start a fight
I made sure you look happy throughout your day
so all your friends can look in amazement and say:

Surely he has the best woman in the land,
a strong woman that is consistent with her plans—
the one who satisfies his every needs,
she must be in charge of that bedroom "breeze."

You Can Find True Love

You can find true love
If you just open you heart and say:
Come what may; I will go
To a land that I never know

No short cuts to spoil the plan
just count your steps on your hand
The higher you go; the harder you might fall
but its better to risk something than nothing at all

Faith will lead the way
Just ignored what darkness has to say
The deeper you travel; maybe nothing yet!
Then all of a sudden Love was sitting calmly upset

So glad to see you; just tired of getting wet
Finally true love is home; no need to fret
As we hold hands and face the unknown
Knowing that God would not let me manage it alone

I Wanted You First

As I watched you, my heart begs.
I immediately got guarded and crossed my legs.
I was not sure what you wanted
but in your eyes you looked extremely hunted

In your there I could see
you making love so gently to me.
I heard your heart many times skipped a beat
the minute you caught a glimpse of my treats

In the depth of my soul, I felt bold.
between my legs, I was shivering cold.
Just the thought of you wanting me
put my entire body in a rough motion at sea.

I knew with you the ride would be rough,
but my hot soul was born tough!
I was worried that I might not be enough,
but I relied on my confidence to make a successfully bust!

Strange enough to me,
I was the one wanting to lead,
so glad I took the chance.
I knew I had you hooked from your first glance.

Hard to Say No

I deliberate planned on telling you no
but my heart, soul, and mind didn't want to go
My mind wanted to resist for sure,
but turmoil began as my heart was unable to endure.

My soul was the aggressor,
confident; not the negotiator,
restless; my mind yearns to believe
what's beneath that wet seal

My mind stood like a soldier, brave and unsure
While my heart sang sexy songs,
Arousing my soul's interest; causing
a relentless chase that persisted.

Sure enough, my heart said stay.
My soul had conquered and took over that day.
My soul agreed with that sexy song
as my heart kept singing.
Sexy tongue is where you belong.

Sex

I know I want to have sex with you
Just thinking how to be more than gentle;
knowing it's all about you
I want to see the enjoyment in your eyes with tears
telling me that you are happy to be mine

Enough passion to make you feel security
and make sure all night you receive the majority and more
so many kisses I have for you, so many hugs to put all over you
tons of lips to scoop up your tears
I don't want to miss anywhere!

Pressure to fit the mood, only if you say I could protrude
I want the intensity to fill the room;
only if you allow me to fully go through
I will push only if you I say can
and stop when your voice gets mad!

I would love to kiss your toes and with your permission
I will work my way up to your sweet mansion
I will stop only if you beg please
And proceed with a sign of relief!
I respect you!

Midnight Romance

Candle light, with warm embrace
as I pass the back of my hands down your face.
Sweet smile with a glass of wine;
you would not believe what's on my mind!

Mini dress with legs out, long slit
at the back of my mouth.
Sweet smells-- down there
I hear that dripping underwear.

Soft music, dancing in space,
emotionally in time with the milky waves.
Sweet words will take off your shirt.
No words—I will take off my skirt.

Red rose I will change the rest of my clothes
All night we will be doing different pose.
Sweetheart; bubble bath
You are an awesome piece of art!

Wet lips; let's kiss; between my sexy tits,
get set; ready, go - I am about to explored!
Smooth legs spread across the room,
dancing and wiggling on that broom.
Wind blows; energy flows
all through my one window.

Please wait! Can you come late?
I promise not to lock my gate.
Strong hands down my ass.
Let's aim to make it last!

Good night. Thanks for the bite.
I was so hungry coming off that flight!
Deep breaths; raising my chest
What took you so long to caress!

I am sure

I am sure about us
I don't care about petty fuss
I see the bigger picture with you
People talking all the time
Please look my way and be mine

I have never been so sure in my life
Today I will commit and end all strife
The world would sorry we didn't give in
To foolish pride and gossiping

I am sure I want to walk down the aisles
And continue the million and more miles
Sign seal will only believes
I will show you as I roll up my sleeves

I never second guess myself
Only if I see something sitting lonely on the shelf
Full of dust I ought to know
Where have been; maybe dreaming looking out my window
So soft I can finally see
You were always deeply in love with me!

Men & Love

Will I ever understand the thoughts of men?
I have spent ample time with them.
Different names, same games.
They never seem to accept any blame!

To express love is seriously forbidden.
They will go through many loops to keep it hidden.
Love may not be buried in a man's heart.
sometimes in his private part

I have tried to figure how men think!
Confusing ways; cannot find the dam link
I might be able to conclude
his love might be hidden in his bizarre moods
.

A man may express in the strangest way.
Don't be too quick to become dismayed.
Try not to be too busy like a bee,
it's easy to miss his attention key.

Late at night when he wears his special cologne,
this is just one of his ways to show his funny bone.
I guess a man's love is never plain,
but you will definitely know the first night after sleeping with him
.

Don't forget a man takes the time to know a woman's soul and
a woman takes the time to frustrate a man till he is old.
A small token will not confirm his love is somewhere there
because his love might just be floating in the invisible air.

Learning to Love

Love will teach me how to examine myself
so I will not accumulate dust on my lower and higher shelf.
Love will teach me how to submit to my other half
so I can bond and create a peaceful path!

Love will teach me how to prepare my lover's meal
and how to ask him his opinion; please
remembering to show courtesy,
incorporating diplomacy.

Love will teach me how to make love.
Timing will be sent from above.
Love will improve my mind,
causing me not to get left behind.

Love will not tell me whose duty to do;
because life is screaming that's why we are two.
Love will teach me how to nurture my young ones,
making sure the next generation is equipped for the next round.

Love will not take any shortcuts.
It will teach me how to have guts.
Love will not let me skip any steps.
It will allow me to retrace and correct my mess!

Love is the greatest teacher of all.
Love sometimes will let me fall.
Love will tell me when to give up my dolls
so I can be fully ready to walk down the hall!

Love will teach me how to refrain from gossip
and have conversations that will only profit!
Love will teach me never to jump to conclusions
but to find a logical solution.
Love doesn't have gender.
Love always signs its name *surrender!*

Women Are Special

Please, mother! Tell me if I am wrong!
And don't add power to make me strong.
Encourage me to improve my masculinity
so I can better handle the world of femininity.

I want to treat my lady with respect
and not punish her with words of defect.
she is the nurturer of man
It's the reason why I can proudly stand!

Why is my woman's heart filled with hurt?
tell me something so I can use as reserve.
Explain to me; that my woman is like a flower,
and if I don't water her, she would wither!

Please tell me to take my lady to dine
ordering the most expensive wine!
Mothers always insist the woman would be fine
Until something happen; then the man is left waiting in line

Whenever I come home and complain,
tell me to be a man and state my claim!
Chase me out of your house with a shout!
Tell me to be a man and not a mouse.

Remind me that I hold the golden key
and act with responsibility.
Tell me I am the provider of my house,
and quit being louse!

Tell me that my lady and I are one
and she's not a toy just to have fun!
Tell me the truth when I knock on your door.
Tell me what makes my lady's heart sore!

I know I have a special lady in my hand.
Help me to straighten up and become a man.
I don't want my relationship to become a bent tree.
Otherwise I would be drinking sugar water for tea!
I came out of you with the breadth of life.
I am looking to you for the best advice!

Please Touch Me

Touch me here! Touch you where?
Touch me there! I guess touch me everywhere!
Run your fingers under my feet
as my eyes close and I retreat.

Pass your lips against mine,
While I gently let you inside
Let me feel those hands that smack!
Just beneath my lower back.
Use the penetration of your fingertips.
Reveal the strength that's in my tits

Pour some oil between my towers,
making them rise up with powers!
Place your teeth at the tip of my soul;
it's okay! Please be bold!
Caress the sweetest part of me,
allowing me to see double in disbelief!

Roll your eyes up and down,
indicating that you are ready for the next round!
Hold my hair with the strength that's wells up in you.
Pull with discretion, according to the mood that flows through.

Arrest my hands, and read me my rights too!
Blow a kiss and tell me it will be long till you are through.
Spin me around like a top; squeeze my butt until I pop!
Look into my eyes and ask if you hit the spot.
I will reveal I am dying to drop!

Ignore all distractions that knock the door;
don't even listen! I just want more!
Keep me nailed with the spikes underneath the sheets;
don't release me even if the blind man weeps!

Romancing

Let's remain in the dark even when dawn shows up,
pushing back the hands of the clock so the momentum would not stop
keeping the vibration through the air; keep it coming;
hope you can swim, my dear!

Wow! Please cover my lips;
I don't want the neighbors to catch a fit!
I can't tell you how many times I've been there and back;
I keep thinking you will finish my water pack!

Every time I think I am finally there,
you turn me on with those sweet words I want to hear
Hold me close as my body goes into a trance;
sprinkle your water; while I dance!

I can't tell you how many times
I've dreamt of this day, picturing us playing games
I feel like I've known you all my life!
I am glad we were able to manifest this love at last.

Let me be the one to arrest your soul;
let me blow some ice and freeze you ice cold.
Let me run my tongue down your lower back.
I want to freeze that forbidden spot so you can relax!

Expressing My Passion

Let me play my favorite song;
and passionately make love to you all night long!
When dawn comes and says we are late,
I will just show it my thirsty gate!

I am a beast when time tries to fight.
I'll break every rule in sight!
This lovely cool night belongs to us
When dawn see us making love it will stop and trust!

This is an opportunity to grow
A chance to taste your world;
just allow me—I have something planed!
I will use more than sex to uncover this man.

Let's not rush this night; I am enjoying your sweet land.
I am in charge; exploring this handsome man
I already told dawn I don't need the light;
I see clearly when things are not so bright!

Turn around and let's start to play;
I see the time is saying six o'clock down there!
You are sweeter than grapes freshly picked from a tree,
sweeter than the honey from those faithful bumblebees.
I like the smell of your breath, my dear,
even in the morning when your storm sits near!

Roar like a lion; don't be afraid to shout!
Bite me using your "Dracula mouth"
Expressing myself; wild and passionately
It's okay if you look desperately in need!

Whenever I Look at You

Before we consult the covers
I want you know you will always be my lover
All over my body; ready to receive your kiss—
I will closed my eyes until you crown me princess

Passion will always be on our side.
Lighting candles as the sex gets more than wild,
As our love energy becomes trapped between.
Not even the wind can intervene

Pleasure is felt from every angle.
I have private thoughts about a romantic triangle.
Anything is possible with us;
our relationship barely encounters any fuss!

Our body was open from the start.
I was prepared to risk giving you my heart.
I'm so in love with you.
You are definitely a dream that was promised and came through!

When the Heart Cries

As the tears poured out of my soul,
my entire body ran cold. I still can't forget
that night, overwhelmed with sweat.
These feelings are killing me.
Till now we never disagree!

I have other responsibilities;
The things you have done has distracted me.
So many questions as the pain persists—
you just up and took away your kiss.

What I'm supposed to do?
Just move on to number two?
Sorry, buddy—not yet!
Karma will be on that same jet!

You might not be here today,
but I know you will be back someday.
In the morning when you look out,
the sun will cook you in your own pot!

I am not forcing your emotion
I don't believe in love portion
I think I am the best so far;
There was no need for these unwanted scars.

I saw all the possibilities,
and I listened to everything you said to me.
Hurry and come before this poem is done.
Every day, I fall out of love before the sun goes down!

Love Pain in the Morning

This morning as I was awaking,
I could not feel the breeze's stroking
All I knew—it was another day of horrific pain;
I had to endure once again!

The love held me, arrested my heart crying in need.
This love caused me to bleed.
My future is at stake, how will I succeed?
I will have to make a 360 degree

My love took over the driver's seat.
I was so powerless; I felt beat!
I remember meeting you; laughing down the streets.
I enjoyed participating in your private retreats.

I ask myself how I must define love.
Maybe I thought it would be without flaws
How could love be so sweet today?
And bitterness all over the next day

Love woke up this morning and did not smile at me.
It never even drank a cup of tea.
I will stretch out my arms and give love a hug
just to test to see how strong is our bond!

I heard so many rumors about you!
But I kept a straight face as I rally through.
So much gossip and we are not married yet!
Is this the red light that's supposed to make me sweat?

I will close my ears and dry my tears
Going the extra lengths I will rid my fears.
I will not force my love on you
because then it would just defeat a dream come true...

Come If You Love Me

Would you like to visit the unknown?
where there is no guarantee, not even a phone?
A place where anything is possible,
but only if you are willing to hustle!

Each day you will experience something new;
it will even give you blues!
Not to worry; we will reach the sky
way before you think to die!

There will be days you will want to quit,
and life will say, hurry up and do it quick!"
It's not that life does not care;
it's just that life has no room for fear!

Some days you will not eat!
Maybe you will have to beg your neighbor for a treat.
There is nothing to be ashamed about;
it's just part of the darn unknown route!

In the morning when you rise,
you will say, "This is not wise!"
I am packing my bags; this place is not for me;
it's for people who believe in eternity!

As I look in the distance on the cloudy days,
I heard something say, "Being a coward pays!"
I said in my heart, "Not this time;
I am determining to see the sun rise!"

I saw what life was trying to do—
making me feel guilty so I could pursue!
Really life does not care;
it's just there to show you how to bear!

We Will Make It

Good morning, my love; how are you?
I did not hear you come in! Are we through?
I was wrong about what I said during yesterday
can we regroup and go over everything once again?

I am so glad I found you in my nest,
honey! I promise I will make
an effort to do the rest!
Come on and don't be shy;
you are truly an amazing lovable guy!

You kept the bed sexy and warm for me.
You deserve all my honesty.
You make sure the locks are firm on my heart
so no one can pierce it with a dart!

You are always willing to meet me half way.
You deserve for me to come along the opposite way!
You always saturate the air with love for me to feel!
Don't you worry—you can trust me!

Let's kiss and make up.
No time to focus and linger on petty stuff.
Allow me to rebuild your confidence.
No need for you to put up a defense.

Your Spirit Spoke To Me

As I stood in stillness of the day,
I felt your spirit trying to penetrate its way,
asking for an invitation to come inside,
then my heart begs the question?
Do you want to talk to your guy?

Trying to convinced me it was not so
and the intention was not just to go …
Circumstances beyond belief
swept you off; leaving me in grief

There was nothing to accept
but obey and go to the next step.
I am tired of missing your tenderness!
My soul thinks it needs it for happiness

I know we will meet again, and
this time it will never end.
Secretly hoping you will wait for me,
but in the meantime, let's just
let everything be …

I love every part of you.
Even your sexy unusual hair does
The nights are lonely; I wish baby, you were here!
To spend some time to show you how much I truly care

When the Love Dust Settles

When the dust settles, you will see
I was the person who came for us to be …
You did not really see me for who I am.
You just looked at me with a double-crossed mind …
never took the time to search deep inside.
In a million ways you indirectly said, "Be mine"

Then before the dust settled, you took off
You ran when you encountered the first bus
You did not even look back to see
the bruises that you left behind for everyone to see …

I shouted with all the members in me
trying with all my strength for you to see
Yes! The chaos was almost too much to endure …
but I was there shouldering you when you wanted more.

In two seconds you did not know me;
you traded me for a so-called opportunity.
You left sure for unsure, not stopping to think!
You would be back for something more;
I thought you would stop and take a peek,
down the road, where success unfolded so neat.

You allowed your present circumstances to cloud your mind,
and you walked away and left me behind.
You took everything that was truly mine.
Your conscience one day will give me back every dime
It will also inform you when you are asleep
you should not have taken that senseless leap!

Until then, I will close my eyes so I can see
And keep on believing in my dreams
My love life will not stop because of you
The clothes you left with were completely torn.
Right then, I knew something was immediately born …

You were in a hurry when you left;
you forget the tools that kept you dressed.
When it gets cold, you will feel
the love you denied right before me.

You will remember those love tugs,
and right then you will miss my genuine hugs.
Until then, I will let everything be; broken and blatant for you to see.

Your Eyes Tell All

Your eyes answer every question that arise
I can tell when you are afraid of losing your prize
You never say I love you so, but your eyes say,
If only you know.

If you were sad and don't want to share,
your eyes would say: Please help me; I am sinking here!"
I know when you feel alone,
because your blinking signals me to know.

I know when you are having a good day.
You pace the floor and say,
"Let's do something impulsive today!"
You always take those crazy routes,
the ones that frightens me, and inject doubts!

You never focus on the troubles of the day,
because you are constantly busy, looking to find a way!
I know when you hate my funny jokes;
your eyes sit still and say: don't make a note!

When you're mad—well, everyone knows.
Those eyes say, "Let's not go down that road!"
I always follow your eyes as a guide;
It's the loudest place I can find!

The Highest Value Reside Me

You saw the highest value in me,
something I could not of unlock with my own key.
You cause me to believe
that the world is always sitting at my feet,
waiting to lavish me with treats.

You took the time to look deep within my soul,
to find out what I was really worth.
You held up your magnifying glass
to see the smallest detail; to know if we would last.

As you penetrate deep inside, whispering "Be mine."
I felt so secure knowing this love was divine
You extended your heart for me to see
That my highest value was
embedded way beneath my negativity!

I really thought I was buried and long gone!
But when you came, I believed someone could
see beyond !

What I Am Feeling Now

I was happy when darkness came
because I knew I would be reborn again.
I think I allowed myself in way too deep;
now climbing out, but the my is falling asleep.

You held the key to my soul,
and yet you never took the time to know
how hurt I was when you left,
how my mind was in mental distress,
how my body ran cold, how all my members wanted to go!

At that moment, I thought to myself,
I have to do something before the twelfth
was it a toy show all along?
Were you just waiting to be ripened and be gone?

Today I will look for my eyes
and take charge as soon as the sun rise.
I know I would make it before the twelfth
It will be the perfect opportunity to replenish myself!

The only thing I regret
is that I got too caught up in your ridiculous net!
I wish I could turn the clock around
and run faster than any sound.

When I saw your face with cheer,
I knew you did not want me there!
Why else did I not sit with your friends?
Because I know you just wanted to pretend.

You worked so hard to encourage me up.
And right away, you had no problem watching me drop!
Today I will get my feelings under control
and stop letting the world know!

My love is too precious to run outside;
without clothes, I would surely die!
My heart was placed in your hands,
but you crashed it before we reached the wedding dance !

The pain was so strong, mixed with flame.
I looked many nights for something to make me sane,
something to uplift my soul,
someone to me take me out of this hole!

A sign to lure me into the sky,
a sign to show me I don't have to die
in every pain there is something to achieve—
with this experience I was able handle more grief!

Me

I am juicy; tastier than a freshly pick orange
It's where I get my strength and courage
I manage to rebuild my confidence
As I painfully gave up a life of pretend

I lived a lie for many years
Just hiding to show some fake tears
The burden got heavier by the day
I eventually learn to shine my own light;
Removing all of my fears

I was a prisoner of my own soul
making excuses just not come home
I wanted to please the crowd
Just so I would not have to bow

The first time I receive a real kiss
It healed me from my brokenness
I immediately wanted to leave the world of vanity
And return to my favorite place of reality

Now from the outside looking in
I will never trade reality just to win
I am happier living in a real hole
Than a mansion filled with priceless gold

Allow Me

Allow me baby to offer you more
The minute you walk through that front door.
I understand that your back must be sore!
And you need a woman's touch to get to that core

Allow me to take all the disappointments away,
And give you a pleasant appointment today.
Allow me to intensify the atmosphere
Let me return in one minute bare

As I am rubbing your labored shoulders
I can't wait to bury you under the covers
As I reach inside your mouth,
Gently pulling all of your stress out!

Tonight I will be your stress therapist
and prepare a warm bath I would not miss
Surrender yourself to me
as I relax you and set you free

Allow me to fix the damage
Let me show you how good I can manage
Smooth and gentle wiping the sweat away
Let me straighten those eyebrows so they can look my way!

It's obvious that something made you gloomy.
Relax here, while I give you, my magic smoothie
Honey, whenever you feel distorted and in a bunch,
You can depend on me; I will have your stress for lunch!

Invisible Love

Love came to me in the month of November.
I kept my mind clear so I can remember
I did not want to accept your token,
but love spoke and convinced me to be open.

Changing my clothes a million miles from home
Your love convinced me while I stayed in Rome,
pouring that favorite wine all over my chest
created a sweet sensation on my breast ...

Experiencing that feeling of security,
seeing our relationship with clarity,
knowing that you don't always have to be physically here
to engage in hot romance and still be elsewhere

Having sex with you while you are far away
I should have started when you left for that trip back in May.
It's never too late, because I found a way
to remain satisfied while you was temporarily over the bay.

Lovemaking in the absence of the flesh,
kissing and having invisible sex ...
Can be truly the best!

The Bliss

You must not resist the bliss
It's extremely important----because you might miss!
I know everything seems abnormal and unsure
but the universe is trustworthy; standing by the door

You should follow that intuitive bliss
It's your inner man; telling you this!
Second guessing is not your place
Stand confident; otherwise you can be easily replace

Everyday promising to change your life
But when the bliss comes; there's always internal strife
How long will you live a life of complexity?
When the bliss gets down on its knees?

A Wonderful Man

Sometimes I just don't understand
Why I am so in love with this man
Unique and strange, he has always been
I am the only woman that internally knows him

It feels good to know someone is trustworthy and around
Even in those bad days, when my behavior is hell-bound
His ways is so balance and profound
During the years I was hardly left with a frown

When the streets grew envious of me,
saying my behavior has been so ungodly
he always showed how nonjudgmental he was
This man never takes revenge
His natural instincts is to defend
How romantic; he is definitely fantastic!

Dinner for Two

Excuse me! Table for two
waiter please! I need you!
Red wine will be fine;
bring the finest for us to dine!

Sweet perfume blazing up the room;
Oh my! I see a future with you!
Nails groomed, make-up lights—
Waiter, please bring us some red candles----bright!
Sexy dress makes me stare;
please come and sit closer my dear!

So when the sun wakes up, what do you do?
I am a professional, how about you?
I am a relaxed man with a straight face;
I am the one that determines my days …

Compliments are on me;
I am the gentleman you dream to see!
Oh! A real woman is in your space;
I am here to expand your business with grace.

I built this business with the rawness of my hands.
Sorry! I am not trying to step into your shoes;
I figure it would be great, since we are two!

It Takes Two

One hand cannot deal;
you were sent to compliment me!
I'm impressed you recognize that!
Let me roll out that red mat!

I feel the same way too.
I feel the need for a man like you:
strong back, arm like that;
I am happy that I sat!

Look at the night; it's shining extra bright.
Waiter, please! Another bottle just like that!
Cheers to you before I met I was blue

All right, let me get my pen.
I know you are ready to sign then!
You are brighter than the morning star.
Don't change a thing; I love you as you are!

I have come a long way.
I would love for you to stay.
Let's take a walk and talk by the bay.
I did so much traveling just to find
I felt many times nothing was mine!

It was worth the back and forth
along with the lengthy route.
Many times, I kept a long mouth!
While my heart battled with doubts

Nonsense! Life will never play foolish games.
Life never deviates from its golden rules!
Thanks for reminding me; it's so true …

A contract is full of important tools
and if you miss the fine print you will look like a fool
Asking life for a gift comes with gain—
Commitment along the way with pain!
Congratulations on trusting life and yourself,
You diligently held your end,
Now life will be faithfully extend

I Need You

You are an interesting creator with the perfect heart
I'm hoping and praying that we never part.
I love to taste your morning kiss.
The strength of your hands I miss.
When it gets extremely tough
Your personality strengthens the both of us

I can't imagine life without a chance
Even with your faults flooding my ass.
How do I make you feel secure?
That my love runs deep and pure

Breakfast, lunch, and dinner too,
I want to spend the rest of my life with you—
working out problems in the dark,
growing old passing our parents mark

No trouble is hard for me to endure.
I have been back and forth through that same door.
I want to make you happy some more.
Allow me to my to pour

I feel proud when I stand next to you.
It's like a woman good and always new.
Your tears make me believe
What my naked eyes cannot perceive

I want to go outside to let the world see
with all your flaws, you are the one for me.
I am not afraid of what might fall out from the dark.
I want to join you in your sorrow till we laugh.

Someone told me once if you fell into my lap
I could have you until eternity comes back.
We both need fixing here and there—
May be more fixing on your part, my dear.
I would not leave you in the dark alone.
Because I just love your funny bones.

Tough Love

Tough love always resides within;
it's the feeling that demands more, and can handle pain.
How do you expect not to tear?
when you keep taking off your underwear?
When in doubt, take another route
or close your legs and stay wrapped up on your couch!

Why sell your feeling short; pretending to be real?
Your life will continue to wobble like a ditched wheel
Easy love is easily given,
Tough love is always hidden

Having trouble getting back on course?
you took off so quickly talking about divorce
How many times the sign came to see
and ask a zillion times: would you like to listen to me?

Hurry up and pack up those sheets
if you want things to start running sweet.
Don't give in even once more;
that might be your last tolerance at the door

Take the key to your heart and hide it far
until you see something above your set bar
You don't have to wait for a light to see;
your intuition will allow you to sneeze!

Follow the pull within—that's the feeling
You don't know its name
Trust this important part;
it will lead you completely out of the dark

What's your method for fixing your game?
I bet it's built around secrets and shame.
Change the course before the light gets in;
Otherwise you will be fighting a losing game.

Hold on to integrity, and you will surpass this route;
don't get stuck trying that mental workout!
Leave all the work up to your guide,
that warm feeling that burns on the inside ...

Tight rules are in place,
but ask life; it will give you grace.
Holding back is a legal part of any game.
It's the most important process that brings you out the flame!

Trust Your Decision

Here I stand with tones of uncertainty again,
doing the same thing because I am so vain!
Trying to move forward in the dark,
trying to remember when I first start.

Each time I make two steps,
I somehow seem to forget;
I wonder if I am not ready yet.

I give up that old life a long time ago,
and it's time I seriously let go!
It really does not do me any good;
It's just makes me feel like I should.

Maybe deep down I am thinking I made a mistake,
and somehow I'm trying to regain what was taken.
Life said to me: "It's either you are in or out!"
Don't make confusion on your own route.

Allow change to bear; allow change to treat you fair.
Give change space to work.
Stop hindering life; don't be a jerk.
How long is a string?
As long as you believe within

The decision is done and can't be reversed.
Let life assist you with this difficult note.
If you begin with the end in mind,
you will graduate from being a complaining child.
Everyone has their own plate;
don't focus on if you are going to be late!

Every step is the next level up,
even if you feel like everything has just stopped!
Sometimes stagnation seeps in, and life will use
anything to get your attention on the way!
Procrastination has rooted itself in you;
just be glad that life was part of your decision too!

Tell Me Why

You left this morning without a trace
Was afraid I would never see your face
without saying what you were about!
I wanted to kiss you, but you ran out

Why do you give me the blues?
When all I wanted to do was love you?
Hold on to me; let love flow.
Just take my hand and never let go

Why it's always about you
Complaining that you are never happy;
and we are through
I want to go the lengths with you;
I want to have copies; more than two…

Why you always think things will stay the same
Mistakes are there, waiting like a game,
so it's okay to bow your head in shame,
I will not judge, because I'm just as guilty as you.
I will not fuss, because I want it always to be us …

Why you took away your warm embrace?
Many nights I felt the hot,
steamy tears ran down my face
When I met you, I wanted to marry you right away
I knew that the very same day

Just don't stay too late, because this poem is about done.
Hurry up before the bittersweet morning comes …

Love Me for Who I Am

Life is about give and take,
To not sacrifice will definitely be a mistake
What's wrong with the pants I wear?
Oh my, you always complain it have so many tares!
What about when I made you that hot morning bath?
You could not even see through that!

Gladly jumping into bed without a kiss,
Signaling that you deserve all of this!
Your face is always broadening with smiles;
but under the sheets you barely looked into my eyes

It's so hard for you to face
that I am truly the opposite of disgrace!
Talent and skills are seasoned in me,
I was blessed with uniqueness for the world to see
Support and credit are always under attack.
Judgment and cruelty you tend to put at the start.

Lucky for me I trust me,
and I will not allow these criticism
to penetrate my belief.
I will finish what I start;
because my life is properly mapped

The universe will never waste time on me;
every pain was designed to help see.
My breadth had me booked,
my troubles would yank me out like a hook!
Even though the sharp edges left some scars on me,
it will often remind me of where I used to be!

It's up to you if you want to share your dreams with me;
I don't want a high off of becoming free.
I know we were meant to be,
but I can't slow down my life to make you see.
Forcing is poor taste; flowing is given by grace.
I only want to flow with you
through the river where no one knows!

Each day my life turns over a new fold;
I am not the least worried if some parts have mold …
Promise me you would love me for who I am.

Your Love Is Enough

It only seems like we are far apart.
You are the only one that has nurtured my heart.
Today someone lent me a kiss,
but you are the one that I miss!

I told them your name is romance residing within.
The keys to unlock my heart are hidden
To leave you is seriously forbidden
Here and there bruised but I will never refuse.

You are my best friend since June.
I refuse to go through life without you.
We survived our troubles on that noisy block
because our love was solid as a rock.
I will prepare the dinner and save you a special spot.

I will not spend another morning alone.
Today I'm not waiting any more by the phone.
You belong to me, and I'm not waiting for you to see.
I will just cause my belief to bring our life into being.

Unique Qualities in You

You possess strength and ability.
I am turned on by your vitality
I often laugh over your hostility.
These qualities are your fuel for our mobility.
I'm impressed by all your capabilities!

Our love life burns like fire.
I intend to stay wired.
You are the only one my heart desires.
When I am around you, I feel inspired.

I will continue to follow this bliss.
My soul willingly wants to persist.
Even when I am pissed,
I will look at you and kiss.

You have been faithful with your continuous devotion.
My entire being is often filled with emotion.
I feel like I was given a love potion!
I know the universe will give our love a promotion.

You Left Too Soon

Some opportunities last for a year.
Others just don't even bother to bear.
You went after a dream with a cute hat …
but wisdom told said you would be chasing a cat
so sad that you could not see all the beauty
that you left behind in me!

When the shame comes, it wears no clothes.
It will all happen under your nose.
Exposed things will pose
And the door will already have been closed

Shame is always looking for someone to blame,
and it walks purposefully with an aim.
Life is a wonderful work of art;
it knows the perfect path.

Some opportunities stand extremely close;
others are the perfect clone.
you use your eagle eye?
and borrow the turkey that stood by?

Eagles are constantly flying in beliefs.
Eagles will see the trademark behind the hidden tree.
The peacock fooled you with its clothes
Or did you forget a peacock just likes to pose?

Mistakes are made always is a rush;
that's when everything is camouflaged in a bunch.
Everything takes time … patience works closely with the divine …
Why ride an unfriendly horse till you fall
when you can ride safely or not at all?

I know it's only been a year,
but productivity played with us till we bear.
Life was in our favor till you left,
but you were too scared to take the next step!

Believe me, love is hard to find …
and it will cost you more than a
charm mimicking a dime!

I'm Excited about You

Your excitement calls my name
even when your face remains the same.
The smell of your perfumes lures me into the room.
I'm undressing as I follow you.

Every time we make love, I feel like bearing two.
I picture them looking exactly like you.
I understand your weakness that creeps.
I know how to play; the knowledge is mine for keeps.

You say you didn't feel for me,
but in my presence you were on your knees.
Your actions didn't line up with your words;
when we made love, your heart was heard.

You kept my hands on your chest.
In my mind, I didn't have to guess.
You felt safe and secure
At that moment, you wanted nothing more.

Let Him Be

When you tell a man success is on the right and not the left,
he will challenge you, cutting off your very last breadth.
Telling a man the streets will make him old,
will just push him further to walk alone!

If you tell a man that the oak tree
will not grow until many years to come,
he will look at you like a little girl sucking her thumb!
Try convincing him that he has to tilt the land before it can bear,
he will tell you that you are infecting his plans with your fear!

He will immediately shut the only door of fame,
not realizing the importance; presently being played!
No fault of his, just the world around,
filling his head and keeping him bound!

The only way a man can see; is if you leave him to bleed,
allowing him to fall on his own weight,
leaving him to experience his own disgrace!
The only way for a man to stand
is if you stop trying to help him adjust his plan!

All the potholes that are in his plan is
enough to groom him into becoming real man!
Let him get to the end of his rope;
let him go through when there is no hope!
Don't catch him when he's about to fall;
Only if he sincerely calls

Don't try to take the sand out of a man's eye to see
until he lets you know that the gravel is making him bleed.
Try not to intervene!
Never convince a man against his soul
you will dance to the same song until you both grow old!

Unknown Love

Nothing makes sense to me.
My heart is begging for an answer, please.
Come, honey, sit here.
Let me show you how much I care.

I am afraid I will forget the times well spent;
my heart is getting terribly upset.
I never wanted to hold you back;
I just felt I could not relax!

I felt like someone close to me had died;
as I moved forward, I began to cry …
My heart tells me I will see you again,
but I am unable to know when.

We did not gradually break if off—
you just took off like a wild horse!
I kept running after you to see,
but your action insisted, " stop following me!"

Those words hurt me to the core.
My heart screamed; I could not handle it anymore!
Hurting me will not make me go away.
I was born to fight especially when I feel dismay

I got to know you during the course of the year,
enough to know something just doesn't feel fair.
I can't place my finger on it now,
but I intend to find the answer somehow.

I went back to our special place, looking for a sign;
I could not find what was once mine …
For days I tried looking between the lines!
But I couldn't find the truth—too many lies.

I will remain a soldier in pursuit,
tracking you down; I will not stay mute.
I have a loud voice in my heart,
And today I will trace back everything from the start.

Sweetness

When your kiss pressed against my face,
the warmth of my body quickly melt with haste.
I saw all your inconsistencies—nothing new—
but you balanced it by keeping those meetings too!

You never stopped me when I poured my loved on you.
You got mad if I did not adore and continue to
Yet you were not patient enough to stay with me;
There were too many prospects on top of you like fleas

As my body ran cold, everything seems to be taking a toll.
I fell in love with you because you were fair;
I trusted that you would always be there …
I wish it was easy to erase you from my mind,
but I guess it will take more than just time.

So many questions and no answers yet …
in the meantime, I will admit I got wet!
All my friends told me to let you go,
but I knew what went on behind our closed door!

You blamed me when life was uneasy;
you told me many times you felt sleazy
My heart was suddenly filled with tears,
running water, bathing with my fears.

We have to regroup again,
because you did not tie up your loose ends.
The chapter will remain open till I know …
admitting that we had a unique relationship tied tightly with a bow

Don't Hide from Me

When I turned the lights on, you were not there.
I didn't want to believe in the dark you stood bare.
In denial you hid your shame
To manipulate my love that was so sincere

I knew it seems that life was not true
Life tends to rough things up when you are rude
training you to overcome and stop being crude …
is love first golden rule

Why did you leave in the middle of the night?
Were you afraid I would start a fight?
I calculated you were keeping secrets from me,
but honey, I would never have taken back the keys.

There is nothing you can't do or don't do to stop my love.
I will stay with you even when times are tough.
I am not afraid of the sea; I will challenge the roughest of the breeze

I would never judge you, big or small.
I will look beyond the chaos; and ask: Why didn't you call?
my heart remained filled with curiosity;
I will forgive you for packing and abandoning me …

I looked and your clothes were not there.
I pretended that I didn't care.
I cried every day, overload with fear,
but my love was anchored; my heart didn't tear!

I Love You Inside Out

I love you inside out.
I'm trying to avoid a drought.
You thought that life had closed the love gate.
The minute you turn your back, life said wait!

I gather you were just filled with fear,
and you didn't want to hear,
fearing what I might think of you inside,
wondering if I would leave you for another guy.

There are so many men on the front line,
but you are the one I'm happy to invest my time.
Our conversations are in sync;
the lovemaking is better than a strong drink.

Now that we have sorted out the truth,
It feels nice to be deeply root
I will not force you to see; I will let you think and be.
Just know I don't have doubts or fears.
I am faithful with my words, so I do care!

If it's love you are after, here I am.
You can count on me to execute any plan.
I will live with you, laugh with you, and marry you,
all because these are all the things that make you, you.

We Have Each Other

There are so many fishes in the deep
I feel honored that you choose to be with me.
I often wish upon a morning star
to fall in love with someone just as you are!

I would not trade you for a soul.
I will stay in the rocking chair till we get old,
and if you get sick before I sleep,
I will bundle you up, keeping you warm in the sheets

We have only traveled half the world so far!
Today let's pack our bags and follow the morning star!
We don't need a ticket to pass.
We just have to show our love will last!

We don't need fifty people to be happy!
With two we can have our own party
We can create our own songs,
loving each other as we travel along!

I Enjoy a Strong Woman

I love a woman with a strong mind
A woman that can see the hidden
details that make a man blind,
and when life treats me so unkind,
I want my woman to stand firm on the front line!

I enjoy a woman with an open mind,
not a woman who is lagging behind.
Some gentleness to balance all of this
She must be sharp and will hardly miss!

She must be swift to plant her seed on time.
I am looking for a relationship
that will create never-ending vines!

A woman who understands flexibility
and possesses a character of dependability
with a love of certainty
and a mind that withstand the times of testability!

A woman who will stand by her chief
and will agree in the things that his heart's believe!
Soft, smooth, and flexible too—
each must be securely assembled you!

Smooth Woman

It's so easy to read your mind.
I never have to wonder or rewind, because
your eyes are always filled with the signs.
I never have to wonder why

I often get a positive instinct
with the right idea; I will link.
Then all my negative thoughts just go extinct.

Our love is faithful and kind
it's hard work, but I would not resign.
We have come a long way; we are refined!

Today I feel like I'm on cloud nine.
Honey, you are my earth and sunshine.
Your body is the perfect design.
I'm so happy that you are mine!

Last night I called the airline
so we could go to a place called the alpine.
There we will be naughty and confined
all night drinking expensive wine!

Please Commit

We have traveled thus far on this bumping road,
dragging naked through the cold.
Sometimes you seem so distant,
and if I try to reach you, it causes resistance.

It feels like we live just to coexist.
Maybe you want it so, making it easier for you to exist.
I feel like you have placed me on your waiting list.
so hurt, I have my tears to kiss

Why is it so hard for you to express?
I get stressed when you keep me in suspense.
Sometimes when I wear a pretty dress,
I can't tell if you are impressed!

I spend all my time treating you like a king,
but I still feel far from wearing a wedding ring.
You often smile and say, "Next spring."
Please don't view our relationship like a permanent fling!

I made sure everything was fine.
I took off all my clothes on time!
To let you know I love you the most.
In my heart where I held you so close!

I Feel Secure with You

I love spending time in the countryside
where we can make clear decisions and decide
Your hand's caresses; keeping my heart from being torn;
You always start this from dusk till dawn.

To be away from home opened my eyes.
When you are relaxed, you became my honey guide.
As we spent time on the mountain side,
I felt like my mind was being detoxified.

I am happy you became my bride.
All my life, I had trouble expressing what I felt inside.
A lot of the times it was my pride,
but now I feel there is no reason to hide.

You are so adventurous and ambitious.
Nothing about you is fictitious,
just wonderfully and so delicious

I often get confirmation of your love.
I want to wear you like gloves,
above the sky to a new height,
wishing to never come back,
just remain with you out of sight!

I Love a Strong Man

I'm enticed by a strong man
so when troubles strikes,
he will tightly hold my hand.
I enjoy a man that thinks quickly
and will not hand me a stick that's slippery.

I admire a man that has a battle plan
and can execute on demand,
a man that stands confident; boosting with sure
and will make me feel secure.

I hate a man that likes to skip—
lying, making up different scripts.
I love a man who stands by his word
so when a storms hits, he
will not take off like a bird!

It's really sexy when a man uses his mind
to choke a strong wind that's unkind.
In a man's heart holds the masterpiece
I think if I softly press it, his love will be released.

You Know I Love You

Where should I look for advice?
I don't want to be seen as a mouse
I often go to the neighbor down the lane,
but they always expect me to be in pain!

I am looking in the wrong direction?
All I want is genuine affection.
Today I will drown myself with liquors,
because I am tired of being your brain picker.

Show me where the answer is resting.
Is this some kind of testing?
I need to get to the other side
where I can replenish my pride.

I guess it's okay to be confused
and lay in bed enduring the blues,
to know love is sometimes unexplainable,
to feel love is truly remarkable.

Today I'm going through a new phase,
and I'm not in the mood to play any games.
You told me that our love is secure
and you promise it would not hit the floor

Our relationship is like no other.
You mean more to me than a brother.
In your hands I placed my life.
I just want to eliminate all strife.

At times you would wear a mask
only an excuse to complete your task.

Settling Down with Me

Is it me, or is finding love an art?
I was thinking maybe it's a divine path!
Do I have the skills to manifest this dream?
Yes! The great one has already injected a beam!

Follow the light that says go slow!
Immediately the part would begin to flow.
I am in doubt; I want to let go!
That's why sometimes you will never know.

Is that the truth or a figure of speech?
Yes, that's why sometimes you just can't reach!
Too fast you would not be able to grow.
Maybe you and a mushroom might as well elope!

No! I am destined to grow; surely that will not be me!
I am dismissing doubt—you just wait and see.
I expect to fall in love because I confident in my beam!

Please Stay

I was shy too ask you to stay;
I thought I frighten you away!
How desperately I fought with me,
battling to stay above the sea

You were quiet, and I did not mine.
I just wanted a hint or a sign.
I looked for an answer on your face;
it just appeared blank; not even a tiny trace.

I struggled to figure you out
My heart threw a tantrum about
I contemplated if I should open my mouth
How do I ask this man out?
I wanted to avoid one-night stand
And be able the next day to call you my man

Men and women are like kettle and pot;
I think after all I might have a shot!
As my boldness came toward your face,
fear just went back in its place.

Would you stay the night with me?
Sure, honey; my heart was sitting here saying please!
I am glad I didn't think twice
I trusted myself as I toss my dice

Beloved

I am alone without you.
My world is so noisy sometimes.
I feel so blue!
When you are close, the journey feels right,
so painless—not even a fright.

I feel like the world is sitting at my door,
Still can't help but feel ignored.
My life doesn't feel complete;
I am working on those edges that need to be neat!

When you are here, my troubles are afraid to come.
They lay in wait hoping for the sun to go down
They know that you possess that sharpshooter's gun!

Your presence is like a consuming flame.
The ones that don't belong are exposed to shame.
Negativity is always looking for someone to blame,
but I will use love to beat it at its own game!

I am happy when miseries go to waste;
it plagues me when they don't see your face.
Your love is positive seeds.
I'm so motivated to go forward cutting down weeds.

Let's Make Up Baby

As I ventured through the living room,
I felt unhappy; I knew I was doomed.
I found myself wanting to hide
from the woman who promised to stand at my side!

I can't believe I was being drilled
by the one who said she would keep me filled.
my body yearns for that thrill.

Sometimes I can't wait for the day to be over to tell!
but before I start, she begins to yell.
It's feels like a constant tugging in my heart.
I wish she can change into something sexy?
before we drift completely apart!

The external pressure has cost me my day.
I wish I could come home to hear her say:
"Honey, I love you, and you deserve a treat"
Let me turn you into a sandwich so I can eat!"

I often wonder if she can read my mind. Maybe she
will change into that something sexy so I can smile.
Some people cannot see farther than their nose.
I probably should have at least bought her an authentic rose!

Maybe it would introduce how I feel,
because I am not good at expressing these love genes!
I have trouble revealing myself,
but when you are mad, I feel like an elf!

If you would just take the time to see
how frustrated I am in these construction jeans!
You are my butter cake.
I would do whatever it takes.

Hush now; reaching over with a kiss,
let's stop this foolish shit!
It's okay, baby. Now we see!
We just had a moment to disagree to agree!

Secret Thoughts

Oh, sweetheart, I desperately want to wake up with you
beneath the oak tree, so we can talk things through.
I want to constantly see your morning face
I just want to love; not a moment must waste

I will follow your soul wherever it goes,
even in the depths of the underworld, you know!
I love you so much; I choked with speech—please
tap on my back so I can speak.

I get so confused when a question arise,
the words immediately begin to attack my ass!
Whenever I open the window
the birds sweetly come and encourage me to stay

I know it's silly, but I would risk,
closing my eyes, and have faith!
I will use my creativity to play
and open my heart and hear what it says!

I told them I cannot make it happen faster than it can;
I tried before and got completely thrown into a can!
I am not going to skip anyone who is ahead of me;
I will wait my turn and see!

I know it's a silly risk to take,
but that's my creativity-task; I will have faith!
Art never made any sense to the naked eye;
it's really for the ones with an eagle eye!

I want to hide my face in the wall
so if he enters, he will not call.
Every day is a risk I am sure,
but my heart reminds me to let life lure!

I Am Here for You

Honey, please don't use pride.
You and the world would constantly collide.
I want to shield you as you carve your way,
so the ride will be smoother the rest of your stay.
I miss you way before you are gone,
thinking how I can protect you from every storm!

I want to see you buzzing around like a bee,
singing only sweet melodies.
You deserve to assimilate the benefits of your life,
because you never give up without a fight!
You were always contented along the path
when everyone fought with you in the dark!

I want to be there when the thunder threatens with fear,
attempting to depress every New Year.
I want to help you win the war
that beckons you to come out and roar!
I will be here flying above the sky,
continuing to watch with my eagle eye!

You Are My Left Hand

You are my left and I am your right;
we need each other in order to fly this kite!
As the wind pushes against our nose,
we will looked at each other and think, *Suppose …*
We are unstoppable without each other,
but we are a fireball when we are together!

We can handle any confusion along our path;
before we came, we were assigned this part!
Let's get to work and do what we came here for,
fulfillment as we advance to mature!

Assignments are not given without rules,
and along with them, we will cater for the blues!
There are napkins inside the traveling bags;
just don't make them hinder our plans!

This is not a sand castle we are building here!
This is a mansion that we have to bear!
There will be distraction all around,
but that will not keep us bound.

And I didn't come thus far, to create a dilemma.
We are good partners are par
We dripped day and night, soaking wet.
There is still a way to go; our harvest is not yet!

A Strong Relationship

As I feel my way, approaching the door—
that's when everyone starts knocking more!
I dare you to ever answer that call!
There's only pain and resentment waiting with claws!

I am not opening up to be stretched apart;
I am going to continue carving my art.
There is still a lot of work to be done
before the harvest date comes!

Let's continue working and not deviate from the plan;
distractions are sent from across the land!
Just focus on the plan with the end in mind,
keeping your head angled toward the sky
as we use our eagle eye!

Folding into a cushion if anyone should fall,
shielding each other from the predators around
as they lay in wait with their tongues drooling along,
waiting for our guard to be let completely down.
Sticking to the plan is the key player in any game.
I know we will navigate faster once we don't care about shame.

My Soul Loves Me

My soul speaks to me every day,
pleading that I should go the other way,
banging on the door to be free.
My soul begs on its knees.

My soul thirsts, wanting to try something new.
We are like husband and wife working things through.
My soul is brave and strong.
It stands up for me even when I am wrong.

No one can stand this faithfully.
This is between my soul and me.
We are one and nothing more.
Our love will never walk out the door.

Every morning when my soul rises,
it blissfully wants to give me many surprises.
I am always in rush,
pushing just to get on that damn bus!
Leaving all the fun behind
just to go to slave in someone else's mind,

Leaving what's real to chance,
forfeiting the opportunity to enhance!
My soul sometimes grieving with so much pain,
yelling daily for me to come out of the rain.

My soul is always anxious for change;
it understands the importance of different levels of games.
Swiftly and constantly seeking a new way out for me,
whispering soft words of harmony so sweet!

My soul thirsts when I am far away;
it desperately wonders when or if I am coming back some day.
I once traveled the dusty road far from my soul
Wearing myself down as I pre-maturely grow old

For every simple question, there is a simple answer.
At every test, the soul knows what's coming next.
My soul has all the answers waiting for me....

Sometimes I am afraid to hear what my soul wants to say.
not sure if I am prepared for the answer today!
I really need to commit to my soul
And listen to where it wants to go

I know I am as young as I feel,
And my soul is just wants to keep it real
I think I'm sometimes afraid of myself.
I think I am sometimes afraid of tremendous success!

The Man I Married

Hey there! How are you? I could have sworn
I had this conversation with you.
Were you the one I married before we were born?
I remember because you had that same tux on!

We spoke about this relationship
and how we would encounter hardship.
You spoke about when I fret,
and we said the foundation is not solid yet!
Are you sure you can't remember me?
I know I am not wearing my usual!

You remember the joke you told me about that diamond ring!
You said you would be happy to be my king
We laughed and talked all night long.
You were frightened that I would not remember somehow.

We promised each other that we would never forget.
Please try to remember, because I'm getting upset!
You always told me that you love blue;
And you wanted me to bear you two!

We promised to build the mansion above the sky—
enough space to fit each child!
We talked about each other's hurts,
and we devise a plan to keep everything chirped.

We knew that our families would not agree,
but we went ahead and hid the golden key.
We kept it safe while we traveled apart;
I knew we would need it when it got dark.

I feel the pressure on my heart;
it's like someone throwing darts!
What else can I do for you to remember these acts?
Maybe we should ask time to send us back!

I wonder if it was the route you took!
I remember my father told me to read this note:
"By the time you both get there, my love,
he will not remember you as his dove!

Okay, I remember my dad saying give him time;
he will be just a little behind.
On the way, the cloud rested on high for a while.

When opportunity knocked my door
I quickly rose up and open so it can tour!
I am anxious to know what life has in store for me.
With all the negativity I just didn't believe

Oops! I forgot I planted so many seeds.
That's why I hear buzzing all around like bees
What a sweet sound!
Today I know I was found

I'm Free in This Relationship

I came into this relationship independent of you;
I came with all my tools.
My eyes are there for me to wear;
it's legal for me to stare!

Okay! What about when you are not there?
Can you still control if I decide to have an affair?
I want to change the line of clothes I wear.
Not even that! You think is fair!

Trust is the ultimate
Use it so you can have peace
Carry it where you go
Especially in times when I am long away from home

Trust can give your self-esteem a work-out!
So there should be no need for torment with doubt.
I think our relationship is solid as a rock,
but your negativity constantly remains a block.

I'm confident in my womanhood
and I'm not confused about if I should.
I really need you to be on the same page with me.
Otherwise we will not be able to reach the letter Z!

Give Her Space

Tonight I decided to go for a stroll
to get my thoughts under control.
I felt the handcuffs on its way!
To arrest my soul; I was determine not to fear!

If I wanted to go to jail,
I would have blown out the bank manager brains!
How complicated is this relationship going to get?
I am so distorted, and we have not set the wedding date yet!

I think most issues are fixable,
but each person has to be willing to let something go!
I came into this relationship with some basic needs.
We can look past this and proceed.

Did I miss something before we started last May?
Or was I caught up with you calling me babe all day.
Can we step back and see what can be done?
Every morning I am waking up with a frown.

Confidence, ambition, and patience are independent rules.
If you don't possess these qualities, you can consider yourself through!
We need patience to manage our relationship
Along with confidence and ambition inserted perfectly like a chip

What I Am Really Thinking

In the depths of the earth, I lived in the crust,
inhaling constantly all the musk
just to build us a house.
Secretly in our circle of doubt,
In our house you boldly treated me like a mouse!

My heart aches silently every day,
but my smile became my crutches along the way!
Many nights I held on to my balls.
It is the only thing that prevented a fall.

It is the only thing I have left that defines who I am,
so I must be careful that I am not disarmed.
I have placed my dirty ways in the fiery fire,
cleansing daily what your heart didn't desire.

It is a daily battle I must fight just to stay alive;
otherwise, the lions would not have their midnight fast!
I was born with the basic tools,
working diligently to buy you those dainty shoes.
It's never enough! The same song that burns—
You don't understand the battle field is hotter than sun!

Gorgeous angels pass me by;
they just wiggle with a devil's smile.
I am tempted to go every day,
hoping that they may be able to ease my pain.
Many days I drove home in doubt;
in the traffic I found myself giving a shout.
Same game different pain
I don't want to stay on the road to gain!

I Love Having You Around

It's been so long, longer than time knows how.
I got so used to your aroma around.
Many nights I tossed and turned,
thinking about you as my heart constantly burns.
You were mad before you left.
I said good-bye to you, but you played deaf!

Many nights I tried to fuse,
but you transparently refused.
I was left alone in the dark,
afraid of the reality; as we part!

In between the sheets, I called your name!
I thought it would have cleared up before
I literally go insane!
But you continued to drag it out.
Insisting that I zip it up!

I wanted you to convince me that no one sneaked
while my eyes were open I still peeped
Slowly I came to the room
There she was dancing on your broom

So sad, yet so glad
I realized you are not a man
I am impressed, I don't have to guess
I accepted I was deeply in love with a piece of mess

I gave you the coat off my back
but you just continued to lack
For years you treated me worst than slack
and I still came out the winner after those brutal attacks!

I often retreat into my private thoughts
Where I spend time working back and forth
When I climb above my favorite tree,
I can see everything you are doing to me.

You let my heart sit on the floor,
As begged not to be ignored
Quiet miss, as someone else embraced your kiss
Unanswered question, why did I allow this?

I can smell your breath from miles away,
the same smell that always makes my day!
Many nights you left me for dead
Excuses freely pouring your head

You are the strangest creature I have ever met.
Sometimes I wonder if I should have taken you to the vet.
You are not the average man that walks about.
You made the love impossible to open its mouth.

What Every Woman Wants

Every woman wants to wear wedding that ring and grown.
It's her dream for it to drag gracefully on the ground!
Anxiously waiting for that special kiss
that will tell her he wants to commit…

Going to family dinner every week,
trying my best to fit in with those fancy retreats
How much more do I have to gave
before he can hand over his last name!

I walk and talk with class,
carrying myself up to mark!
Being careful never to offend,
I have perfected the art of how to blend.

I always remember to say hello to the queen of the day,
making sure the respect doesn't fall by the way!
I want more than her approval

I want him to make a decision based on only me
and don't mention the words "but she"
Many times I feel like I have to inject my claws
Just to keep my future in-laws off!

Time! Time! Time is so precious
I wonder if he knows;
this is my life, not some cartoon show!
I am not surprised that he is not ready yet;
Good thing I made room for his twenty percent!

Chance

I still gave him a chance
Despite many times feeling it was his last dance
It wouldn't hurt to give him another month or two;
hoping he knows after that; we're through!

I wanted to know if this was for me,
so I took off my fake lens to see.
One night I ordered the most expensive wine
just to see if I could find a genuine smile.

It pays sometimes to wait;
because slowly that night I saw more of his traits!
The opportunity presented itself for me to know
That it was safely time for me to let go
Sure enough he didn't agree
That he cheated on me

The minute denial removed away
I recognize that his dirty ways will continue to stay the same
To change a habit is a choice
He would never stop even if I scream on top of my voice!

Why Look for Acceptance

Why punish my being looking for acceptance?
I really should trust my subconscious
Some people are only happy when things go right;
And that red light lets everyone knows it time to fight!

Life is like a graph.
I will just connect the dots and follow my path
The graph will always tell me where to go.
So my problems will not continue to grow!

Too busy trying to impress the other side—
that's because I know what they are really thinking inside!
I know there is no real love there, and I know
when I am in the dark, nobody shows!

Waiting for someone to offer a cup of genuine tea,
but all I hear is "hurry up I must leave"!
Constantly looking for that support,
I will never find it on this bankrupt route.

Too busy wanting everyone to see
Too busy; I kept forgetting me!
The one that holds my hand each day;
The only one that says: I'll stay…

Too busy looking all around,
busy bee trying to belong,
I kept thinking that somebody
is going to confirm my song.
I found the hard way when everybody
was quietly long gone!

See

Why can't I hurry up and see?
they don't believe that I can be
They saw me with a broken car;
anticipating I would not go very far!

How can you continue to be?
I am struggling to believe
If I can take the clouds away from my eyes,
I know I will be able to see clearly outside!

It's a good idea to constantly feel my way through;
I just have to stop putting my feet into those stinky boots!
Sometimes I want things that I can't have
The things that doesn't have any hands

I am constantly viewed under a different light,
hoping that I would not shine too bright!
Acceptance doesn't want to be my friend.
The game will only get harder if I continue to pretend!

They doubt I possess the tenacity;
they thought I was born not to be!
I will shift my focus to the other side.
That way I would stop being blind!

I will be happy for what's on my plate;
I am grateful for good grace
Long eyes don't reach very far.
A satisfied heart will match the given bar!

What Is He Really Thinking?

Yesterday I felt like moving in with you
as I was dressing for work; putting on my shoes.
When you first asked me, I hesitated.
I was afraid that you would be my soul mate.

Every night I would think of only you,
pretending I am dancing with you on the moon.
I am sorry I made you sad.
Forgive me and don't be mad.

There is not a day that goes by when my heart doesn't cry,
but my soul strengthens me, saying, "don't die."
I regret the hurtful things I used as reasons.
I know I created a rough season.

I saw the love in your eyes.
The move I made was not wise.
Meeting you was like winning the lottery.
I so regret using you for your money

Each day I had to live with guilt.
My conscious is pressuring me to rebuild.
Allow me to mend that broken part.
I'm seriously ready for a fresh start.

I saw love and didn't care
I want to make up for not being there.
I know I can't reverse what took place,
but my heart is humble and yearning for your grace!

I Want the Keys to Your Heart

His face was blank without fear,
only a line that signaled that he was doing okay.
On my knees, I begged him, "Please,
water me with your love because you hold the keys!"

I caught a glimpse of the keys to his soul;
I am desperate I am about to get bold.
How safe does the environment have to be?
For you to sacrifice your entire heart to me!

My mouth springs water every day,
hoping he will open up and say:
here is my heart; I've placed it in your hands
I am the man that can strongly stand

I love you, but I don't believe
that you will forever give me the keys
I have done everything possible and more,
but it's that commitment I'm looking for…
I appreciate every ounce of sweat that you have invested in me!
I am thinking you are having internal conflict giving the keys.

It's Hard to Win His Soul

He appeared like he did not care!
But I followed my heart as it led!
His fear was that I would find someone else,
knowing his behavior never made sense;
but still he did nothing to change,
He just kept treating me the same

I guess at the same time he can't believe!
A woman who would love him despite his deceit
He used his attitude to cover his shame
causing the lonely nights to feel the blame

Maybe it's easier for him to pretend;
Guarding his heart until he decides when
Watching and waiting; with his eyes close
Sleeping is the furthest thing from his nose

Honestly, it's hard to win his soul
And get him to open up and stop being cold
He hides his feeling in order to see me
Not giving him a chance to believe

I will be patient with wisdom
And wait for life to give me that thumb
Trusting the path and myself
That love with not leave me lonely sitting on an empty shelf....

Choosing the Voice

I am not listening to the voices that protect,
trying to keep me from getting wet!
I hear the voices that are extremely calm!
Not the voices that sound like a farm!
I hear the still voice say, "Today love will rain
Leave your umbrella just joins the walk naked …"

The calm voice keeps me asleep,
while the loud voices makes me weep
it easy not to get confused
guarding my heart so I would not get used

It's good I have chosen my battle field
being sure not to sleep with the server and the sheep
wanting one, without the other knowing its two
the responsibility will always be on you

Trying to figure out this risk
Just riding this unborn twist!
Life will definitely send me the bill;
I can't leave because I will get kill!

It takes pleasure in giving different kinds gifts
Sometimes those risks are not worth it
I will follow the voice that says go slow
because I don't want to risk I will never know…

I Still See Your Face

I can still see your face
where we met at our favorite place.
I remember us having long talks,
holding hands; going for walks.

In the morning when I rise,
I can still see the love in your eyes.
Touching every part I reveal
I was surprised; I can still feel!

In your face, I see what's real.
I'm holding on to this belief.
In your face, I can see the truth.
I see our love still buried at the root.

When you left, your face came with me,
reminding me of what was meant to be.
I know I must keep our love alive,
because it unwilling to die.

I never forced your face to stay.
It voluntarily came the next day.
Your face told me I should not stray
but follow love—it knows the way!

I am Thinking about You

Each day I think you are best
Regardless of how many times you have made me stress
Whenever you touch me with your warm lips
The sweet sensation burns, but fits
As your breast sharpens with looks that are true
Nothing is fictitious about you!

When I close my eyes, I can see you clear
How easy it is for you to find your way down there
Nice and cozy I will come inside
I was so thirsty; I had no strength to fly

I thank the universe; it never makes mistakes;
it's important that we see each other again.
Even though tomorrow you will not be here,
I know I will feel your energy everywhere!

I am so eager to see you are not gone yet,
but I will ask time to have the future arrangements set;
I will blindfold myself and take many chances with you
because there are many beautiful women,
but the genuine hearts are so few.......

You Will Regret

You will regret the day you traded me for sex!
It was so easy for you to say next
I allow you to take the lead,
because I truly believe
this love could have lasted a lifetime.
but you ignore the calling signal and signs

How many times the feeling
whispered and you purposely resist.
When you met me, you were the one that persist,
you judged and doubted what was real
waited too long for life to revealed

You walked away from true love,
which you will not find lying about!
I was innocent and with few flaws;
You were just greedy and decided to look for more.

Bounce your ball as you see fit
Just watch and prepare for that hit
a love like this comes once in a million years
so you can drink and down your sorrows in beers

This love was extremely rare.
This type of love you will never again wear.
In your hands there was me.
Through your hands, you stupidly let me be.

Pleading that you made the decision before the sun went down,
displacing blame that life did you wrong,
forcing me to believe in your irresponsibility's
buttering up your excuses with in capabilities

I daily looked into your eyes and see
you were the world to me,
feeling sad about the choices you made,
but standing waiting for your childish behavior to fade

You left without a sign,
every day I wanted to die!
One day you will knock your head on the believe
I start using both eyes now to see ...

Love Will forgive

When my life was turned upside down
It took more than a while for me to settle while I was young
Why should I believe your stories now?
You did not leave a good impression—just a frown.

I have worked hard to stand tall.
Please! Not a step closer, unless I call.
Every day I asked myself
how could you just give on our success.
I was left to clean the mess
Let's leave it up to love to suggest

It's obvious you were trying not to see!
What you did was totally to the contrary
Don't worry; I have grown up now.
I made new friends like you talked about
I am still here if you need me,
but this time you must treat me like a lady!

I can't understand why life gives you a second chance.
I guess life saw your efforts from a glance …
The bruises still hover over my soul
As love do open heart surgery, while I'm still cold

I Love You

Before I went out,
I asked the universe for you.
It was the sweetest wish that came true!

I monitored every step of the way.
I saw your inconsistency trying to say ...
This is too much for me; I can't stay
I don't think we would pass the month of May

I love you with all my heart, and
I am afraid that we might eventually apart."
Please placed your head on my knees
so you can feel my comfort so peacefully

I want my giving to be enough.
To fatten your sweet smile like bus!
Other factors might have been in the way;
but you did your best to protect me across the bay!

There were times your energy was low;
there were times I knew you to go
to a place far away
somewhere to hide the shame!

I am anxious to see you again
so we can be more than friends.
In the meantime, while we are apart,
let's mature and enjoy each other blissful paths ...

Trust is the only key
that can fit what was meant to be.
I have placed my trust in the divine creativity,
the only one that can make us who we are!
My love runs deep, past the freezing cold; I don't think a
North Pole can freeze my world.

Morals vs. Ego

I know you wanted to be with me,
but you were too embarrassed to let your family see!
How different I was from the norm—
protecting your status; of course!

You appeared to be proud of me,
but you kept me behind the scenes,
watching and waiting to see
what surprises I had up my sleeves.

You completely went against
your moral side, you use as a defense
Your moral state told you
I was the way, but your ego said, "Hey!
No way! Get out while you can;
stop trying to be a man!"

Your moral side was proud of me,
but your egoistic side said,
"There are more sexy babies in the sea!"
Morality said, "Stand by her side,"
but your egoistic side said,
"Leave her; she won't die!"

Your moral state pleaded with you,
but your egoistic side was so strong too …
Morality said, "Make good choices," but there
again, your ego started to make more voices!

In the end, you gave into your egoistic side,
the one that, don't care a dam thing about your behind!
The ego is all about "Listen to me!"
It doesn't care about the feelings of another human being.

The ego never sifts for right or wrong;
it's only happy when everyone follows its calls.
Soon, when everything is resting quietly, morality will stand tall;
you would then realize you made the biggest mistake of all!

Tonight

Tonight again I sit here,
wondering what happened to our love, my dear!
You told me to move on without fear!
But it just seems odd and unfair!

Did I mean anything to you?
Or was it all about some midnight's screws
You came two and three times a week.
Using me and going out after to cheat!

You looked to me for comfort all the way.
You strongly encouraged me to stay near!
You could have left since last June,
but you decided to continue …

You told me to leave my town
and come closer to where you were born!
I was truly amazed; I was impressed right away.
Then one week later, you said you couldn't stay
So freckle minded I couldn't keep up with you

Quickly you said you had to go.
I felt like someone had robbed me of coat!
I held on to denial for a while,
but I immediately let go and many nights just cried.

Sorrow and fear all mixed in
anger and love started fighting.
As I stand in the middle of the night,
I kept asking myself, did I do everything right?

This Love Will Last

I know this love will last,
because of the experience we had last.
The universe showed me very bold
that you and I would grow old.

The last talk we had,
your heart told me that you were sad.
The energy was so heavy;
it sat right on top of me.
So strong it held me in grip,
making sure I never forget …

All the times spent with you,
I was making sure we stick together stronger than glue,
doing everything so seal the relationship,
placing a strong hedge over this romantic ship!

I never thought of leaving you.
I just think about staying forever and enduring the blues
Despite it all you are still amazing
This romance constantly has me drooling!

.

There is no love like what we share.
There are not many relationships
that take the time to cared
I know this love will last,
because I saw it strongly in your eyes …

When We Met

When you met me, you wanted to dance.
I resisted my first chance
You insisted if I don't you will go!
I gave in, because your confidence let me know.

We danced the whole night long!
You were enjoying yourself all along.
You started licking my ear,
letting me know you were filled with cheer!

I waited anxiously to see if you would call the next day,
but you took your cool time; in my heart I said "anyway"!
I give up after a month, but you
resurrected from somewhere about …

Asking for us to meet again
I accepted; I didn't want to pretend.
I was dying to take another chance
to see if you could bring me back to life
so filled with pain and romance!
This time I knew I would dance

The first time being with you
was the most awesome experience
I have ever been through.
I didn't want the night to end;
I wanted to be more than just friends …

I knew at first you were not sure,
but you kept saying you wanted more!
I saw the trials approaching near,
but I was mentally equipped to handle despite fear.

I felt you never trusted me;
you judged me based on what you saw.
Enticing women blinded your love
All beautiful women was sent from above
You had trouble picking just one

I often wonder about you!
In the end, you doubted everything I do.
The trials came between and tried to last.
But my strength was willing; till it eventually pass!

Our Love Is The Strongest

I know something good is going to come out of this.
I was not just romantic for a slap in the face.
I gave you love and more;
I was there for you when you called.
I never said no to you;
that's because my love was so true

Why do you hide your love from me?
Are you ashamed of what might be?
You can run, but you can't hide.
Listen! My love will never be denied!

I am so confident in my soul
I will share a life with you and get old!
It's just a matter of time before I hear you say
how you love me and you want to start another fresh today

There is no love like mine that exists!
I am a special angel that was assigned to this case.
Forgive me for being rude, but my love for you is not crude.
All my being wants is to share a life with you,
spending quality time just loving you …

I enjoyed the kisses you gave me between the sheets.
I felt the energy whenever I fell asleep!
My heart knows that you are close!
It believes something that no one knows.
Just allow our stories to be unfold…..

You're Here Now

I know your spirit is here.
I can feel your presence everywhere,
stroking my back while I am asleep,
rubbing my legs perfectly,
whispering sweetheart in my ear,
brushing your tongue without fear.

Silently expressing your return,
holding back the tears so it will not burn,
grabbing hold of my soul,
telling me you would never let go!

As you climb on top of me,
your nervousness; I can feel!
You never meant the trip to be long!
But you comforted my heart; removing the frown

Gently touching my toes,
counting them as the days go,
cherishing all the love we share,
looking forward to a better year!

Planning the days ahead,
you are thinking that it's time to wed,
keeping the calendar by the way,
indirectly pointing at May!

May is a special month for us.
It's the month that I constantly
went back and forth; so much fuss!
May sounds like a fresh place to start!
Let's begin by mending the worst broken part!

When the Soul Speaks

I can feel you trying to talk.
What is wrong? Let's take a walk.
I miss you so much I almost didn't bear!
I want to know if you are still there.

Yes, I am here, living my life.
Baby, do you still have a place for me inside?
Why do you want to know?
I am so fed up; you were the one who wanted to go!

I know I wanted to go.
I am sorry; it was not supposed to be so!
Okay, what do you now want from me?
I really want you to wait, please!
Why do you think you are deserving of this
when you were the one who gave me the last-minute twist?

Okay! Okay! I know what I said!
I was trying to get rid of you then!
As the days go by, I can finally see

You are the woman for me!
Why should I believe your story now?
You pushed me away, shouting, "Go now!"
I wondered, was confused; I don't know how.

I miss making love to you.
I am dying to be inside of you,
feeling your safe, warm embrace
Oh, I can almost again taste your tenderness.

I love you so much; I truly miss
your laughter and your wet kiss.
Your lovemaking is the shit!
Am I asking for too much now?
Yes! Too late, the milk already left the cow

What do I have to do?
I would like to communicate in person with you;
I know you are afraid to talk to me.
Do you want me to get on my knees?
You treated me fair and square.
I am sorry I was never there!

I am sorry I did not enforce more cheer ...
I know I hurt you so much, my dear!
I hope you will save a chance for me
that I can redeem myself; I know it's a "maybe"

I Want a Life with You

I see our babies in your eyes
rolling and tumbling; playing outside.
In my eyes, you are the perfect mother-to–be.
I want to show off for everyone can see!

In the morning when I'm awake
I can see clearly your motherly qualities; it's no mistakes
How much you would enjoy our new souls.
I want to grant you this wish as I was told.

When I first met you, I could not see
that we were truly meant to be.
I thought I was passing through a road,
as I looked for something to grab and hold.

I kept looking farther than my nose,
wondering if I was missing something… I suppose!
Not for a short time, but forever you would be mine
The divine creator made you with his hand
I am your matching man!

I am so glad I waited patiently!
The benefits just continues to overwhelm me
Without stopping to make sure
I knew you were my future wife and nothing more!

I forever thrilled that life gave me a second chance,
and you were smart enough and took a stand!
Believing despite all the odds; really took a lot of guts.

Come Back

I want to walk on the beach with you.
I want to go to the church and wed anew.
I can see it in your eyes. How bright the sun shines.
I will be honored to wear that ring;
I will enjoy being committed.

Let's not let the ocean come between
the one year we build was so neat.
Any present faults that may arise—
let's sit and work on them from the inside.

When we met, we saw each other's flaws.
We knew that we were in for the big roar.
It's the reason we stuck so close.
The energy came and bonded us both.

I see the tide rising high,
trying to reach and be with the sweet sunshine,
Let's take action before the flood invites itself in!
I know if we take in front we would win

If you come back; we can work through anything
and heal that feeling of pain….
As the dragons circle in the sky,
I can see the sadness boarding the next flight,

Fearful of what might be the truth,
hoping that it's not you,
wishing that it could be something else.
This would explain this odd mess …

The world is round and I can't find the end.
Everything in it is designed to be our friend.
Even the good that sometimes gets crashed
We must endure till the end

I have searched and can't find
the love that was once mine.
Trying to reach your inner soul,
calling you back before we get ice cold.

Your actions don't make any sense.
I lay awake with no word from you yet.
I'm hoping somewhere in your soul
you will soon recognize my voice and come home!

Listen to What's Inside

In the middle of the night,
I felt something holding my heart so tight!
Pleading and directing my way,
the universe is not playing any games!
I feel the burning sensation in my gut,
stop thinking about that stagnant word called "*but*".

As I walked my merry way,
continuing with my ordinary day,
this constant feeling that I can't bear
just kept tugging on me without fear.

I felt the *but* whelming up inside,
pressuring me to follow this divine.
As I stressed to constantly ignore,
the feeling just continued to build up some more.

I am so used to the same old way,
sun shining almost every day,
rain coming to constantly wash the floor.
Rain coming makes me bored!
The time is drawing near
as the answer keeps tugging without fear.

I try to put the feeling to rest,
but it keeps palpitating through my chest.
How can I ignore the pulling?
that's pushing against my front door,
trying to plead with me,
showing me how to turn this heavy golden key!

Forget the crowd if they get upset;
that's a sign that they are not ready yet!
I will test the waters before I die
and follow what was placed on the inside.

The feeling comes with huge responsibilities
including faith that will sweeten my cup of tea.
The tugging doesn't come with a sweet taste;
the feeling is just the base.
A little whisper is all it takes
along with faith to create the perfect mix

Stir that feeling within;
Just manifest what's awakening.
I will listen and open with the given key, unlocking
the treasures that were hidden for me to set me free.

Nothing Standing in Our Way

Nothing is standing in our way;
love has removed all gates
that wanted to stay.
Mountain high, valley low—
love knows where to go.

To see if our love would stay alive,
I went ahead and took a deep dive.
Knowing that I could not swim,
even though love was not familiar him
I recited my love hymn

Love's tenderness wants to keep us safe inside.
Love's sweet spirit will never die.
Love is superior to any guy.
It will take us beyond the sky.

I am ready to be with you forever!
This is a wise decision—so clever.
I have never felt surer than now.
It's just a feeling; I can't explain how!

Come back to me while the night is still young.
Hurry up before you get stung.
Life already warned, you should not have gone
Sometimes it's not good to go alone beyond

I have placed your picture beside me so
I can everyday feel your sweet energy …
I will send positives vibes your way.
I know it will motivate your spirit to remain open every day.

I realize what we share is so unique.
You are the only one who makes my soul weak.
I will cherish you now and forevermore!
Baby, nothing's will ever block our front door.

I Would Not Tell a Soul

I would not tell a soul
that I have decided to be bold.
These feelings give me the creeps,
but I have decided to go ahead and peek!

I am not sure if I should,
but these feelings are telling me I could.
My natural state insists that I stay sane
and stay away from anything that will drive me insane.

For the past couple days, I've tried something new,
Attempting to keep our love in view
Love asks me to trust without fear,
especially when the answer is not clear.

A lot is being asked of me,
but this love is positively driving me to be.
In everything I must be myself and
allow everything to finally come to an end.
still my feelings say the end is not here yet,
and I should trust and not fret.

It's hard not to fret when I can't see
my sweetheart who was just here sitting with me.
A wind came and swept him on the other side,
but the wind said I would not let him die

The wind promised to return him soon.
He's just passing through to change his banged up shoes.
Hold on to what you believe
and don't stop thinking of what could be
a love that's true and rare.
This type of love will bring him back safe with special care

Close your eyes and you will see
the truth that is unfolding so neatly.
You both were destined to be,
and life is about to post you the key.

I think sometimes I am a fool for love.
My spirit replies, "Oh, no doubt."
Your feelings are real and cannot lie.
They're your lamp in the middle of the night.

I know it feels very dark and vague,
but listen to your heart and hear what is says.
Follow me and you would see all along
why I was telling you to believe!

The soul knows where it wants to go.
The soul will never take the wrong road
The soul has enough faith to tolerate
All the negative beliefs waiting by the gate
It just needs you to trust
and eliminate unproductive fuss

The soul is never afraid to follow its own heart.
The soul wants to be free
from all the trouble and the pain.
The soul is only interested is assisting you to gain.

I Will Marry Him

I know that I will marry him,
because my soul is guiding me from within.
It's hard to follow the way
when everything looks untrusting

I know I will marry him,
because my spirit has showed me the ring.
I am excited to see
what I believed all along to be …

I know I will marry him,
because my soul cannot lie from within.
It's waiting on the other side
To make sure you don't die.

I feel the hammering on my heart every day
telling me I am here to stay.
I feel butterflies inside.
I guess this means, this must be the guy.

Sometimes I am afraid he will not see!
But my spirit constantly says, hey, just trust me!
Assuring me without a doubt,
confident as I continues the route.

My spirit needs me to stay strong,
because that's how my future will be born.
My spirit needs a strong house.
A place to dwell in without a single doubt

I Believe

I believe in you and me
because of what we shared recently—
something special and rare;
I know someday you will be here!

As I lay in my bed and wait for you,
I can feel you contemplating too,
wondering if you should make the move.
Your heart says to give a try
because true love has found you.

This love will always believe
This love is not taking any leave
I believed when everyone didn't;
I cared when everyone said I shouldn't

I will reject all your flaws.
I will only see the good because,
I know my love is sincere,
and I believe when I wake, you will be there.

I will believe when I open my eyes,
seeing your face without any disguise,
you will publicize your real self to me,
accepting what's true and was meant to be

I believe you will let go of this twist
and seal our love with a special kiss.
I will meet you when I open my eyes
And I would have to feel this lover affair was a lie

Holding You

I feel so good holding you.
I knew this was my long wish
that finally came through.
I cried and wished for you every night.
I waited for you to land on that first flight!

I am so glad you are here.
Holding you, my stomach cheers
I want to lose myself in you,
secretly in the bathroom …

As I am holding you, my soul feels fulfilled.
It was starving before you walked in.
I could not wait for your big arms so tight.
I slept with your picture every night!

Love Without Fear

I love you without fear.
I don't care if no one wants to be here.
I can stand alone; I don't need
anyone to let me know
how much investment this took
with this love affair I can write a book

I am not afraid to gamble on this note.
I know in my heart I am going to win.
Even when the odds look grim

The warrior that resides in me
will help me fight to believe,
two is better than one,
because fear comes arm with many weapons!

I am prepared to fight with my belief.
I will stand up strong with a smile,
because I know my soul is at my side

I want to come home and see you on the couch
and not see your panties all twisted in a bunch
Can we work something out?
Let's stop fighting like cat and mouse.

What's Authentic?

Let's make love and have sex
Not because I'm wet means I'm ready yet?
Can you pour me a glass of wine please?
before you start with your tease

Let's talk about, what you love to do in your spare time
Apart from having sex all the time
Where do you see yourself five years from now?
I hope not with your pants all over town

Where is that seductive kiss?
Just place it on my neck, before I make a fist
I love massages with honey oil and cucumbers too
This is a fifty; fifty romance; I'm not through with you

Keep kissing and hugging me
While you remove my sexy panties
Now bring your eyes close to my nose
And inhale my morning breath that blows

Inside you go; just squeeze me tight
protect me as I fly higher than the sky
In between lets romantically dance

You thought it would be easy
as soon as you took off your pants
don't forget to keep your eyes centered
paying attention to a women's needs

When My Soul Pulls

In the middle of night when my soul pulls,
I will know that it's hungry and wants to let go.
I will rise and set off into the dark
knowing I will encounter loneliness on the path!

I will trust the light inside of me.
It will tell me if an invisible rock is in the streets.
And even if I fall, my soul knows who to call.
It will show me how to get my balance grip,
telling me to stand up holding my hips!

The love that dwells on the inside
cares for me especially when I cry.
My soul wants to fulfill its role.
It wants to search to satisfy this pull.

This thirst that's on the inside
longs for its partner to continue this ride.
In the dark, my soul will hunt
in the forest where the wolves are always out!

I will not be afraid of the dark—
not even those green eyes that peep out.
I will ride with my soul to find what it believe.
In the darkness, my soul will never sleep!

Sweet Spirit

As I look to the stars tonight,
I hear my spirit say, "Don't give up without a fight."
It offers to fight my battles every day
and promises to put a smile before I lay

I feel the tension building on the inside of me.
a strong force is penetrating with ease.
That's love moving all around,
with its sweet sound.

It silently moves with force,
telling me that I am not getting a divorce,
inspiring me to hold on without fear
even if it looks the tree looks bear.

I may not see it with my eyes,
but it's not far from the sunrise.
It will be delivered at my front door;
just be careful not to ignore.

My sweet spirit would never waste my time.
It knows how fragile my feelings are within
It understands the love that flows through me.
It would not alert unnecessary!

Every step is calculated and secure.
It's just depending on me to house it some more.
My spirit needs a comfortable place to live
while it works on all my desired interests.

No fake tears on my face.
I will stand like a soldier armed with grace,
knowing that my inner man has order my steps
and all the shortcomings will be met!

So if I feel lost and afraid,
I can rest assured that my sweet spirit knows the way.
I will just follow the next guide.
How simple it must look on the outside!

Love Stood in the Rain

I feel the love in the pain.
I am so glad it rain.
I was afraid it would not last,
because the water had given us an unexpected bath!

We were soaking wet, and I was terribly upset.
I blamed you for not sheltering me more.
I was ready to walk out the damn door!

With your face dripping wet,
you whispered, "Please, my love, please don't get upset.
Let's embrace the storm that came,
as we normally stand; gamed!"

It proves that we are strong
and we can weather any storm.
No bad weather can wash this love away.
I will be damned if I let it any day!

I am here to stay, and so are you,
so stop complaining and see the bigger picture for two.
Our committed love has us standing tall.
It's because of our authentic love….

Bitter/Sweet Love

I love your bitter/sweet voice that speaks to my soul.
It understands everything behind those harsh words.
Even when you are upset, my soul hears the truth in steps.

My soul breaks down your words in two,
explaining your true intentions and views
I am so glad my soul stays awake
To save me from falling off the forbidden slate!

My soul hears the bitterness coming in the distance
It guards and shuns all negativity that tries to be persistence
Your sweet love hugs and kisses all day long!
My soul senses the love coming from beyond;
excited as it worships me, bending down kissing my knees!

Bitterness stands by the gate,
hoping to consume us while we wait
I am happy that love is on our side;
preventing any mishaps from happening; casting down pride

In the bitterness I see the shame, waving goodbye to the graceful wind
standing strong and tall, armless, it can't harm our love at all
Short and low around the curve
Bitterness will continue to get on our nerves

Your Love Changed Me

Your love changed me most of all
And dress me up like a pretty doll.
I felt so perfect; without flaws.
You saw the end before the trouble became more...
You took my hand and pointed success was fun

In the morning when I smell the rose,
you talked about us visiting the sky for new clothes!
You brought tickets for two.
I was not sure if it would come true,
but I saw the certainty in your eyes
way before the sun give us the surprise!

I felt compelled to achieve
anything I wanted to be.
Nothing ever surprises you!
You just expanded whatever I shared with you.

You told me there is no such word as *can't*,
because success is in every man's heart!
You took my hand and helped me reach
way past the scary deeps.
I still was not sure,
but your love made me feel secure.

I trusted you even when you were not here.
Your love was so powerful,
I felt it every way; I heard your
voice in the depths of the deep.
It saved me from staying way beneath.

It always reminded me about the pitfalls that challenge faith
and your love will still be waiting by the gate.
It's a nice feeling to know you are love so much!
Sweetheart, I care about everything that I touch!

Beautiful Woman

Beautiful woman, don't change a thing!
I saw you looking at yourself from within.
Do you doubt who you have become?
Honey, you are uniquely made like morning star
Just last week, I saw you walking down the street.
I saw the men looking at your posture, oh so neat!

A beautiful woman holds her head up high.
You were not afraid to take that dive!
Your beauty shouted, bring it on! You weathered every storm!
A woman is sexy in all different forms,
especially when she can show independence most of all.

What does this mean for society?
A world without beauty will be full of intensity.
Your beauty wears no clothes,
fearing nothing that comes close.
Ready for battle every day,
weaponless beauty will go all the way.

Confident that she will conquer all,
a woman will continue to stand tall.
She will never be short of a knee;
Her life is mapped out evenly!

She shouldn't hide herself from the world.
In its darkness, the world will still know
your light is the beauty that comes from within.
It's able to guide anyone in!

Whenever I looked at You

I saw you at a glance.
At first, I did not want to take a chance.
When I looked at you, my heart leaped!
Because I was not prepared to sleep,

You insisted for me to come your way.
My heart said, "Yes; just stay."
Your aggression turned me on.
I knew a new day was being born!

We danced the whole night through.
At that point I knew I wanted to be with you.
I silently asked my soul inside,
"Please give me this guy!"

I waited, but you never called.
I figured you were not serious at all!
After a while, my soul tugged in my sleep,
telling me to take a peak!
You were standing there strong and sure
I looked into your eyes and I felt secure

I was afraid of being alone with us
But you were a smart man; you never fuss
you softly told me the beach was near
and the loving waters and you will take care
Immediately, my knees started to shake,
I really didn't know what to expect.
My soul said, "Just follows my steps!"

At times I thought I was in the wrong place,
but the atmosphere said, "Hello, pretty face!"
I felt an energy flowing through the room.
I knew that you had just sprayed your natural perfume.

Your energy placed me in a relaxed mood.
You were sharp with me on your first move!
The night felt safe and sound.
I spontaneously danced privately all night long!

You comforted me with who you are.
The trust I felt perfect thus far!
I'm so happy that I met you;
it has been an interesting journey just for two.

We supply each other every day
with enough love and trust all the way.
I would not trade you for another soul!

I will boldly tell the world
how good you are to me
even in the toughest times
when I can hardly see!

I Miss You Tonight

I miss you tonight; I am cold;
I feel like I am sleeping at the North Pole!
Tonight I will light the firewood and pretend to sleep
and imagine that you are here embracing me!

I will sip my coffee and pretend to look at you.
I will stretch out my lips and imagining I am enticing you.
I know the song that puts you in the mood.
I will play it and dance for you.

Then I will go to the window and frown.
I will realize that I have been missing you all long.
Then I will smile and pretend to see you coming from afar,
and I will run into my room and change into something skimpier!

In the bed I will wait for you.
I will keep my body always pure and true.
Red roses everywhere, luring you without any underwear
Now I truly hear you coming in the wind.
My face now has a genuine grin.

I'm happy to see you in the flesh.
Baby, our relationship is truly blessed.
I am happy to express my love to you.
Let me gracefully bend down and take off your shoes.

I know you had a hectic day;
let's start with a massage, because the sun will not stay.
I was so sad before you came and left;
I could not wait to fully express myself undressed!

I Fell in Love by the Pool

I fell in love by the pool.
I didn't imagine it would be someone like you!
I was so used to my every-year taboo,
but my soul said to take a look at you!

My soul told me not to look at your handsome face
but to look way down in that complicated place
where love was on reserve,
fenced around for that special girl.

When my soul spoke to me, it insisted
I must believe, that I am deserving of this love
A true gentleman love is sent from above

My soul wants me to believe
that in my hand I hold a special key,
the key that will take me to that special place
where I would be freed from being restless!

It's amazing when you're not consciously trying to steer.
It makes the adventure more interesting and with less fear.
I was not expecting to meet anyone by the pool.
I'm so happy my soul showed me you!

A Talk over a Bottle of Wine

The bottle of wine is enough for two.
I am sure it will put us in the mood.
Soft music, candlelight; baby, this is no time to fight.

Today I was in a terrible mood.
I am desperately seeking to get soothed
Tired of the same shit every day,
I want to move to the next level; please skip the delay

I only suggested the wine
Thinking it would somehow loosen our minds
I thought it might create a relax atmosphere
So that we can hear beyond each issues very clear!

I chose this special brand around two.
I placed it to chill, thinking about you,
I just want to show you how much I care
so we can talk things over without any fear!

I know you have some concerns along this route;
let's first toast, believing it will all work out!
Cheers to the struggles that we must endure,
cheers to success we refuse to ignored.

As we started conversing in the deep,
I saw your eyes dazzled in disbelief.
In a low, soft tone as your heart tried:
Not too sweet or too dry!"
Baby, you were reading my mind!"

I felt I was already half way through;
I just needed now to convince you.
My intention is always for us to grow,
And not be struggling with mushroom

And when I criticize I want to let you know
is because I love and adore you so.
I see us going past the sky,
but it will take more than just my hands!

I know your soul tells you to take a chance with him,
but you question every time an opportunity steps in.
Close your eyes and take a leap.
You can depend on me; my love is not cheap!

The Heart Never Lies

Take your time; you should go
even if you don't know!
Trust your heart, because it sees
things way beyond what the
natural eyes could believe.

Don't stop! Don't ask!
Just keep walking; trusting the path.
When you see the lion on the way
and the snakes hanging around by the bay,
just keep your eyes on the prize; knowing that
darkness will eventually submit to the light.

Trust your heart; it lives near.
Just quiet your mind so you can hear.
It's speaking every second of the day.
Remember to remove the clouds out of the way.

Trust your heart and don't doubt!
Nobody is better at knowing your route.
Shift your gears; don't be scared.
It will all work out in the end!

Love Is Sweet

Love is pure and so divine;
it taste better than sweet wine!
Please pour me a glass of that better divine
so I can enter and spend time with that man of mine.

If you are clothed with genuine sweet love,
then you are on your way; never to get lost.
calmly walking without riding a horse.

Love has a heart of its own.
It feels pain when you mourn.
It does not dwell in places of disrespect;
chaos is not love's priority anywhere on the list.

Love will not leave you standing out in the cold;
it will light the fire and say, "You will never burn."
Love doesn't want you to sign a loan;
love wants to give you everything it owns.

Love does not give with the right and take with the left.
It brings harmony in the morning until the sun sets.
Love operates in the highest state of excellence.
It only thinks about bringing the best fragrance!

If you get lost you can depend on love,
it will be on your back like a tick on a dog.
When you feel like you have committed your worst sin,
love will not judge; it will comfort you from within.

If you fall on the same floor,
love will pick you up and show you the way once more.
Hold true to love's hands and don't let go.
Love is not puppet show

You will know when you find true love;
you will stay up drinking and laughing loud!
Love is always open to trying new things.
Love never wears a lot of faces,
because love is full of transcending grace!
Love will help you keep a steady paste

It's not afraid of what people might say;
its confident reigning every day.
Love believes even when you are in great doubt;
its sole mission is to pull you out!
Love will sit with you in the dirtiest of shame
when everyone has quit playing your game.

It does not understand the words *give up;*
it will fight with all its guts
Love and success are like brothers,
They need each other to grow their feathers….

Alone without You

I am alone without you.
My world is so noisy; I am unable to hear you.
When you are close, it feels right;
No need to think twice!

I feel like the world is sitting at my door;
it can't be ignored.
I feel like my life is complete—
just those edges need to be neat.

When you are here,
my troubles are afraid to come!
They know you are loaded with guns.
I see them trying to come my way,
but they pass on their merry way.

Your presence is like a consuming flame;
everyone is overwhelmed. I know this is no game!
I am happy to see misery go to waste;
it is plagued when it doesn't see your face!

Your presence is very appeals to me;
even fear knows it and trembles at your feet.
I get excited when you arrive;
With you I will feel comfortable to die!
It's the place I long to be;

Secure; knowing that you will forever be beside me
There are more questions than answers I dare not ask;
fearing my brain will be doing doubting task!
I know by now we should know
that without each other we will not grow!

In Love with Him

I miss you before you think to leave.
Dreading how soon you would up pick those keys.
My heart cries in advance,
wishing the day would last.

I know I am reluctant to let you go.
Honey, please delay and take off your tuxedo!
Its not because of the sex
Is just I am not ready your presence to leave yet!

As my heart begins to weep,
the tears kept flowed uncontrollably from my eyes.
I can't believe I love you so;
the tears keeps penetrating and making heart holes.

As I struggled to hold on;
I thought the love was blind, but I can see
how much I love and don't want you to leave.

It was almost noon; I felt like flying with you in a balloon.
Whenever you looked at me and smiled,
I felt naked in your eyes;
I thought many times about doing a seductive pose.
But I am just interested in dancing on your nose!

How fortunate I must be,
thinking way ahead of me.
His body language made me see:
"Please! Honey, let me breathe."

Stay with me, I bid you now!
I promise to keep a calendar somehow.
Let's make the place warm and safe;
I know it will show on your face.

How delicate your house must be;
let's go ahead and keep it clean.
Hang decorations using stars,
keeping everyone interested so far!

I want to walk down that challenging road with you.
Please let me surrender my soul to you.
Let me help take that block off your track;
holding hands, let us relax!
Let me hug where it's safe and warm,
assisting will shelter you from the storm!

Give me a place in your heart;
I promise I will nurture the path.
Give me a place with your soul;
I will stay faithful like a little girl!

Your Love Keeps Me

Your love lifted the burden when you were not here.
Many times I was frightened, full of fear.
You projected your love over the seas,
reminding me how much you are still in love with me.

In the past, I was not sure.
I doubted you ever more.
Now I feel safe and secure
that your love for me
will rain and there will be no moss!

No more sad face at a glance—
I finally have a happy face at last.
I thought I would never see the day
when you would blow sweet kisses constantly my way

I feel your love flowing through me,
healing all the hurt that you left to bleed .
Your love has apologized to my heart.
Your love was on its knees, pleading for us not to part!

I received your mail yesterday,
and the words jumped out and grabbed me by my hair
Your words were singing a joyous song,
saying, "Baby, I would love to marry you now!"

It's the first time you've expressed your love to me.
I'm in shock and full of disbelief.
All this time, I thought you didn't love me,
and in one day, you've caused me to believe!

possibly indirect when showed your love,
I forever I could not figure it out.
I kept looking for you on the other side,
And one day I started to cry
Then suddenly there was no confusion bundled up inside.
You caused me to see clearly with my naked eyes

All this time, the love was there;
I just could not see. I kept asking where.
At last frustration is out the door
Cheers to our new love life; I want you more!

The Love in Your Eyes

I see the love in your eyes.
It remains fixed while we dance.
You never take your eyes off me.

You undress without touching
As my heart feels you, it start blushing
Your eyes tell me when you feel hurt.
Right away I stop working to take a look,
filling your heart with my love as I remove the pain
so your eyes can be fixed on me once again.

I never listen to the words that come out of your mouth.
Your eyes tell me exactly what you are thinking about
I am never confused about you and me
because I know where to look to find the key!

I enjoy looking into your eyes
because this is where your happiness resides.
Once you are happy, then that makes two.
Baby, I am here; so let me please you!

When you are mad and smile,
your face will look funny, like a little child.
I would never prolong to make you more upset
I would just look into your eyes and retrace my steps!

Apart from being in love with you,
I've also mastered the art of understanding your point of view
I don't see loving you as a job;
I enjoy loving you instead of seeing you sob!

Here We Are Again

Here we are again, just when I thought it was the end!
You somehow told me we would be together once more,
but I never saw beyond when you walked out the door.
I guess because your face looked upset,
I thought you had made up your mind to enter the next step!

Why did you say those words to me
when you knew you would be back?
Were you testing my strength?
You carried on that behavior for many lengths!

I was confused mostly in the night.
But as the days went on, clarity came in late flight,
letting me know that you were so hurt,
and you too were literally going berserk!

You responded to how you felt,
but after one year, I just did not understand you yet!
It's no fun not understanding fully what's in your heart.
The good news is that we were never really apart.

I Will Be Patient With You

Honey, let's take a midnight stroll.
Allow me to love you; let me take control.
For years you mentally fought with me.
Sweetie, two boa rats just cannot sleep!

It's about keeping your independence
because life enjoys keeping things balance
At times I want to keep my distance
and refrain from being persistent.
I understand your temperance,
which is why I will remain patient!

I'm on board wherever you go,
even if it means I have to take it slow.
I'm not in for just for the ride.
I love you, and I want to stand by your side!

Please Let Me In

I know we have just met
and I don't mean to get you upset.
I know for you it's too soon,
but I feel like I know you.

Really, it's not about the sex.
It's okay if you are not ready yet.
Just leave the frowns at the door,
and just open yourself some more.

I understand you just got out of a relationship,
and you are being careful not to make the same mistake.
Your heart is safe with me.
Just give me a chance and you will see.

In the past, I have struggled too.
So, my love, it's not only you.
Together we can make each other feel secure.
And, with time, we both will feel assured.

When I first met you, I saw a person of integrity
the foundation of our relationship heading straight for eternity
I said to my heart, I can succeed at this."
So here we are, standing closer than a kiss
with our faces touching, nose to nose.
I will not give up without a fight
because you have brought a
different light to my life!!

Let's Try One More Time

Your behavior was a handful.
Your attitude was boastful.
The disrespect was a mouthful.
All my feelings became doubtful.

You didn't act like an adult.
With your so-called character came no results.
Finding a solution was so difficult,
I desperately turned to friends I needed to consult.

My soul was uneasy.
Overall I felt upset.
As I finally made the first step,
your actions made me depressed.

It looks like the relationship is through,
but my heart longs to love you.
One hand is weaker than two.
I'm willing to work things out; I'm so blue!

I know our relationship is divine.
Let's talk it out over a glass of wine.
Maybe we just need to clear our minds,
and give it a shot one more time!

Take a Risk with Me

Our love is sweeter than a juicy apple.
Honey, my heart is ready to enter that chapel.
I think I have been more than fair.
You can count on me to be there.

I never treated you crappy.
I will do anything to make you happy.
I hug you tighter than a bear,
so close there is no air!

I want to experience an authentic marriage.
I dream of carrying a baby carriage.
I'm not interested in a common-law marriage.
I look forward to leaving behind this baggage.

We have been dating since June.
I'm tired of hearing your sad tune,
how you are not ready yet,
how you are afraid to take the first step.

Come, walk down the aisles with me
and let me have your babies.
You don't have to feel unsure.
I would do more to make you feel secure!

Lean over and give me a kiss.
And let's put a real marriage on the list.
I promise I will not change.
All I want is a real exchange!

So Beautiful Tonight

Tonight you look so attractive.
My body immediately became overactive
as we made eye contact.
I would love for you to caress my back.

You look so breathtaking.
It feels like filmmaking.
You have heightened sexuality.
I am so thrilled to have you in my reality.

Our love is not superficial.
Here's your diamond ring; it's now official.
This love runs deep past the core.
Baby, you are the only one I adore!

A hug and special good-night kiss—
when I went home I would reminisce
how you were so hard to resist.
I'm glad I followed the bliss!

Love Was Knocking

I heard love knocking at the door this morning.
It's funny; I thought yesterday I saw a warning
preparing me for celebration time
because I have proven I'm able to climb.

How interesting is this?
I was just thinking to dismiss.
I thought love was placed last on your list
or I prayed for something amiss.

The knocking was strong and sure.
I knew love was here once more.
I had prepared my heart for so long.
I'm going to finally wear the gown!

I guess patience is the key.
I know it was not just me.
Love came back and held my hand.
It promised me this time it would stand!

The Bigger Picture

I see the bigger picture.
I know that nature has placed us here.
The troubles make our relationship small,
but in the distance I see us growing past tall.

I'm not afraid to go to war
and be damaged with some hot sores.
Nothing can cloud my belief
because in this relationship I'm the chief.

I trust what my natural eyes cannot see;
a bumble bee is bringing sweet honey.
I hear a sweet melody from afar.
I know it's coming to brighten up the dark.

I'm as sure as the sun will come tomorrow
that with this mighty love we will never have to borrow.
I see life so crystal clear.
Just trust me if you dare!

Focus on what we have achieved thus far,
and let's just incorporate who we are.
If your faith is weak, don't worry.
I will not critique!

All I need mostly is to know you love me
and everything else, and half the job is done already.
Just don't judge what you see on the outside,
but lift your eyes angled at the sun while it rises!

My First Shot at Love

This is my first time being in a relationship.
I thought marriage came after a friendship.
I figured we would date a month or two
before we started going into the bedroom.

I was hoping to fall in love before sex,
but it seems after one dinner, it's what's next!
I would like someday to make love to you,
but I have to be certain that you are mostly true.

I know I can't have all my answers now.
That's why I want to take my time and allow.
Please feel free to express yourself;
don't be like an ornament on a shelf.

I don't need five years to know you.
All I need is to see how you tie your shoe.
People always tell you who they are.
There should be no surprises after sex.

This has only been our second date,
and already you want me to be your bedmate.
I really don't mean to be rude;
It's just that I am overload with value.

I'm aware that we have different minds,
but my guidance comes directly from the divine,
and I am determined to follow the outline.
I am looking forward to telling you I love you,
but more importantly,
I am also deeply in love with you.

Just Relax My Love

Let me make you feel relaxed.
I know you are stressed to the max.
I have just the remedy.
Just shut the light off so I can see

Whenever you are in doubt
and you don't understand what life is about
I'm here to give you smooth healing
And in that moment love will do some serious revealing

Talking things out always changes the atmosphere.
It will feel like the stress is not there.
The laughs will soothe and clear the air
It will surely make you unwind.
Everyone needs that sometime

A little soft music will also do.
It will assist in absorbing all your blues.
Sweet-smelling candlelight!
In the dark where your eyes are so bright!

Your fingers secretly crept like claws,
but baby, I am aware it's yours.
Let me kiss those romantic lips.
Allow me to squeeze your tits.

Let me rub those sexy thighs.
Tell me you feel butterflies
It doesn't get more romantic than this.
Come, my love. Let's do that deep kiss!

Relationship + Work

Today I will pick you up on my white horse
and speed us through this rough course.
I know your heart is strained.
I want to eliminate most of your pain.

Trust me—even if I ride too fast,
all I'm thinking is how to make it last!
I would never let you fall;
I was mentally prepared all along!

I'm always thinking ahead,
because I know sometimes you dread
the future for us.
I pick it up in your fearful voice.

Come and sit extremely close to me! Let's
have a hot cup of tea!
It's so few degrees tonight.
Let's warm each other; it feels right.

It's okay to feel insecure!
Because sometimes there is no
bread crumb on the floor.
I never said this was a magic ship.
Honey, this is a relationship!

You Are Coming

I can smell you coming from miles away.
Your heart told me you were coming my way!
I don't have a date or a time!
All I know is you have made up your mind.

My heart told me to prepare once more,
because this time I would not be ignored,
so I dressed up just for you
and remodeled the place to accommodate two!

Everything is ready. Get set!
I know you are aboard this final jet,
traveling faster than lightning.
My awareness is heightening.

Your light hungers for my light.
All it wants is to unite.
You purposely suppressed what you felt inside,
but true love just cannot be denied!

Friends don't know what you feel,
and there is no need for you to reveal.
I know you are ready to let go all lamentations
and jump right in with all your affirmation!

I Love a Strong Man

Today I felt my face sitting on the ground.
Since you left, I always felt I did something wrong.
I still believe our relationship could be,
even though I feel I'm drowning at sea!

I was always sure of us,
but you created most of the fuss!
I'm used to being independent of me.
Sometimes I feel it was your own insecurity.

It's funny; you always seemed to be so secure.
I guess you saw something in me you wanted more!
Please don't blame me for who I am, because in
my eyes, you are the perfect man!

Let's cherish what we've already achieved
and continue to enrich our soul; don't
let it grieve!
I want to hug and kiss
and jump all around biting your face!

You are my star!
Don't let me wonder who you are.
It's already been five years.
Look! Our relationship is full of zest!
Let's not throw love away.
In this relationship I want to stay!
Strong shoulders to the wheels.
I love you, baby! So please!

You Are Free to Achieve

Honey, go ahead and fulfill your career,
but promise me you will be fair.
Baby, with life's course, just
don't ever tell me you want a divorce.

Someone has to hold down the forth.
I will take a risk and not think about court.
For better or for worse, for richer or for poorer—
these are the lines of a real marriage tester …

Do you think you can pass this test?
It's okay if you are not ready yet!
I'm not fearful of the future,
because the universe always does things in order.

The world is round, and there is no escape.
We are held responsible for all mistakes,
so I will take a chance and let you go
to fly away as I open the window.

You promised that it would only be for a short while.
I will not cry like a spoiled child.
True love has laid the foundation,
and it will ward off any frustration!

I Love You So Much

I will do anything to have you back in my life.
I so want to be your future wife;
I will give you a baby,
but everything right now looks so maybe!

I think of you all night long!
From the early of the morn
till the dusk turns into dawn.

I have visions of your late-night kisses.
I remember those sweet lips.
I remember us dancing in the rain.
Your new suit! You were so vain.

Was my love too strong?
I didn't realize all along.
Do you want to start again with a friendship?
and work our way into a fresh relationship?

I will hold on loosely tight
so you can breath and go on different flights.
I will open my door once more.
We can fix this with our good rapport.

Come back tonight. Not a day longer.
My heart yearns with so much hunger.
I will take off my nose just to spoil her.

I Know What I Did

I will be held accountable,
because I knew you were valuable.
I was never short of your love.
You treated me like the morning dove.

What I did was totally unfair.
My behavior was worse than an angry bear.
I'm afraid you will take your love from me.
And throw away all work on believe!

In this relationship I felt secure;
I never had to look for you next door.
Your kiss always felt assured,
and I was never bored …

What can I do to mend this shit?
A love pill will not fix this!
I know an apology might do,
but it feels for the most part I 'm screwed

This was the best relationship I ever had.
I am so stressed I need a heating pad!
I made mistakes, but I am wondering if I am too late!

I Will Work for Your Love

Sorry is not enough;
it's going to feel like I am building a house.
I am willing to work night and day for you,
because life will not easily
pave the way to let me through!

I wish I could turn back the hands on the clock
and rebuild these stupid blocks.
What a mess I've made.
I have to clean up;
Let me be your maid!

All along you tried to reach out to me,
but I kept playing around with the keys.
I never tried to fix the mistakes;
I just left the relationship to experience earthquakes.

I thought you would always be there
forgiving me because of fear.
I thought you could not do without me.
Now I'm paying for it. Please!

How much time do I have?
I am busy orchestrating a plan!
Honey, I have gambled our love
that was sent directly from above.

I don't know what will do the trick,
but I'm digging into my bag of fix-it.
I feel like my confidence is sitting on pins,
but my heart tells me I'm going to win!

I Admire You

I admired your dignity
and the sweetness of your integrity.
I love you because of those fine qualities.
My space is too small for quantities.

Being with you feels like magic.
To lose you would be so tragic.
I will hide you in my heart
far away; we will never part!

I will play a sweet song
and blow my powerful horn.
Today I have stopped complaining
And I have started celebrating

I have kept the hurt hidden under the sheets.
Sorry, my love; every day, it gives me the creeps.
I know I did something wrong,
but I continue to be strong.

What can I do to make it up to you?
I will give you my love that I have kept in.
I never meant to trample the relationship,
but I saw my behavior wrecking the ship!

Lovers & Friends

We have been friends for years,
and you never saw deliberate tears.
There are only a few people who care.
It seems that you have always been there.

I want to show my appreciation,
because this friendship is truly a creation.
I see us going to the next level.
I know we can fight that mountain devil.

If there is anything I can do
to help make our dreams come through,
I want to work at this just as much as you,
pulling my weight; this relationship is true.

I know enough about us
to understand if we were to have any fuss.
There's no such thing as a perfect life;
I expect us to experience strife.

Our faithfulness has laid the foundation
so the base is fixed in the ground.
Real love will anchor us somehow.
It will assist us after we take our vows.

I am looking forward to a new struggle.
In the rough times we will snuggle.
You and me best friends—
our relationship is not pretend!

Listen to Your Heart

I know my feelings are internal,
and it definitely shows external.
I want our relationship to be permanent,
so I need you to try your best to be confident!

I know I'm hard to understand,
but I'm not a woman; I'm a man.
Just use your gift of discernment,
and you will experience less torment.

Whenever you feel unsure,
just close your eyes and
open the door of your heart!
Trust what you see and feel.
It's your perfect guidance when it comes to me!

I know my ways are different from the norm,
and sometimes it feels like
you are passing through a storm!
Whenever you have a doubt,
just turn to me with love and open your mouth!

Don't keep your feelings bottled up inside.
It would be pointless trying to hide …
I love a woman of persistence.
It makes the relationship have less resistance.

I adore a woman of authenticity;
my body gets overwhelmed with electricity.
A woman who is willing to sacrifice,
Someone that's open for advice,

A heart that's quick to listen and slow to speak.
It's exciting to watch a woman who seeks.
Wisdom is the key to open all dreams.
All I want is for us to be a team!

Let's Disagree to Agree

When I met you, my first thought was that it would last,
but so much stuff has happened; it got stuck in the past.
Every now and then we reflect to see
if our love was truly meant to be!

It's okay to check our status along the way.
It's human to feel fed up, sometimes every day.
It's natural to change our minds as the relationship gets intense.
Just understand that the pain will evolve into a mess.

Separation causes a reality check
to figure out what should come next.
An opportunity to calculate the mistakes,
a chance to see what's at stake!

Everyone feels pains, but everyone
will walk away with some gain.
In life nothing is really free;
the pain throughout the relationship
is the reward we will keep!

I Thirst for Your Love

Today I thirst
only because you are my first.
It's not every day someone falls truly in love.
You are specially made; my lovely dove.

I will cherish every romantic event,
looking back and laughing at the times well spent.
I see us long term; this relationship will stand firm.

I am deeply impressed by your attitude.
I felt moved to show you gratitude.
Your kiss came with permission,
making it easy for me to make my decision.

You only touched when I guided.
You were comfortable; no need to be shy.
No need for penetration; it was an
amazing sensation!

The attraction was the same.
I was so turned on by the flame,
I fell in love at the first stop.
I am glad I ran into you at the coffee shop!

This Love Is Not Over

For a while, I thought it was over.
I cried so much; I didn't have a shoulder.
Many days I search to find
some peace to soothe my mind …

I was shocked you abandoned this.
I never got the last kiss.
Late at night, I thought,
This relationship can't abort!

I started repeating it in my heart,
asking the universe to give us another start!
I slept with your picture to manifest
the faith that I invested!

The time I spend thinking to believe
that we could come together and end this grief!
Whenever I encountered a negative route,
I just would navigate and head south.

I kept my broken heart in peace.
While I meditated and took my ease,
I felt like I was walking on thin ice.
This love has a high price!

I can't afford to pay for it,
because I am the captain of my ship!
I know I just hit a rock,
and our love became blocked.

My strength removes the block,
as our love became unstuck.
My heart is filled will cheer.
Everything feels right; you were always there!

Let Me Show You Love

The breakup felt like hate.
I screamed as you closed your gate!
Your face looked sure.
I continued to scream some more!

Is it because of me?
I refused to believe.
Did you have a fight with life?
Or did life give you a taste of the knife!

Innocently, I got caught in the storm,
all because I was on board.
Please explain; state your claim.
Tell me I'm not to blame.

My love builds our hedge.
Honey, don't throw me over the edge.
Let's communicate heart to heart.
The universe is willing to give us a new start.

Shift your focus; your soul is in unrest.
Come place your head on my chest.
Let my heart restore your mind
so you can stop being so blind.

We have real love in our midst.
Come, sweetheart; let me give you a kiss.
Let me erase the doubt that comes with fear
so I can replace it with cheer,
a joy that will fill you up.
Come and experience what true love is about!

A Second Chance at Love

I didn't tell you because of pride.
I would rather go within and hide.
The truth is I love you so.
I just didn't want you to know.

I wanted to run though the front door,
but love was playing on the living-room floor.
I took a shortcut out of sight
and willfully didn't say good night!

I knew love would look for me.
I took off and left the keys.
Love cried out loud.
I heard it on the other side.
I was not proud!

I felt like I had to abandon ship.
I thought I would wreck the relationship.
I was afraid I would hurt you.
I'm sorry I appeared untrue!

I was trying to protect.
I didn't mean to disrespect.
My intention was not to reject.
I would do anything to connect.

So sorry I was in a hurry!
I knew it would come back to haunt me.
I heard your tears in the middle of the night.
Life once again threatened to give me the knife.

I'm pleading; is there any chance left for me?
I would really like to redeem
myself for all the times I was so mean.

I'm thanking you in advance
For a shot at this romance
This time I will not screw up my chance.

I am Secretly in Love with You

I know you always do all the expressing,
but that does not mean I'm not interested.
Love grew love.
I thought that was enough!

I understand sometimes it feels
like I'm not there; all that was fear!
I know you wanted stability
and not any extra responsibility.

Please understand I have other issues of my own!
But baby, believe me, I don't want to end up alone.
I look forward to spending the rest of my life with you,
crying and laughing all the way through!

I promise to lighten up a bit
and not make things more complicated than they already is.
Tomorrow is promise to no one!
So let's make up and sing; because we belong!

I will make an effort to show more love,
and when you come close, I will not shove.
This love will be for always.
I dream one day to proudly walk down the hallway.

I have searched the highs and lows
just to find a partner that glows.
The first impression is the true test.
The rest will take care of itself.

On the first date, you were so funny.
I was so comfortable, I wanted to say honey.
I felt like I had known you all my life.
We acted like husband and wife.

Our conversation was so balanced.
With a romantic song we danced!
When your eyes met mine,
we knew what the other was thinking inside.

Then came a long 3 passionate kiss
One on my wrist, nose and finally my adorable wet lips
This relationship was no longer in the stage of might!
Because everything felt right

We've smoothed out the rough edges.
Together we build our own unique secure hedges!
Safe for two or more
in case life gives us two little ones to play on the floor!

I saw the future in your smile.
It felt like I had this conversation before I was a child.
This is the most genuine, romantic relationship.

Communication Is the Key

Let's lay naked in the bed
making future plans ahead,
Enjoying each other's company

For a minute let's not think about sex.
Just understand; don't get upset!
Our communication has decreased.
Our sex life is the least.

I hate when you are reserved.
It makes me feel underserved.
You slowly started shutting me out,
causing the relationship to experience a drought.

I feel a bit insecure.
I just want to talk, nothing more!
Would you like something to drink?
Allow me; a candle must be lit!

Baby, I'm just so in love with you
and I don't know what else to do.
Do you feel anything at all?
I fear the relationship is going to fall.

If deep down you think we can survive,
don't continue to deprive.
Please show me you could drive!

Let me see your zest,
not only when it comes to sex!
I know this relationship can grow beyond the sky.
Let's work hard and give it a genuine try.
Talking always makes things a little easier.
It's like a medicine teaser!

You've Been Sweet

I'm counting down the time till I see you.
I get visions every day about just us two.
Remembering how our love is steamy
and how you tasted so creamy.

It was so easy for me to get excited,
my heart was always delighted.
The environment was always inviting.
Your lips always looked so enticing.

You are a dream come true.
I love you, Sue.
I will never again make you blue.
Baby, you have been so great.
I appreciate the drawn out wait.

It took me a while to get sorted.
You did not give up; you fought!
Thank you, honey, for all your support!

Spend Some Time with Me

I get so sad every time you go on those long trips.
It feels like I don't have a grip.
I would like to travel with you.
I will wear nothing except for my sexy shoes.

For weeks you are gone.
My heart burns and longs
I enjoy all your wealth, but I'd rather
our relationship be in good health!

I'm packing my bags,
waving my danger love flag.
I desperately need some attention
to drastically reduce this tension.

Spend some time with my soul.
I feel like I'm turning to mold.
Awake the woman that fell asleep in me.
Touch me so I can breed.

At least come in the shower.
I see you as my only lover.
A gentle kiss will do.
Baby, I really love you!

Your wish is my command.
Honey, you can make any demand.
Is it too much to ask you to stay?
Sacrifice and go the next day!

I need this alone time
to help me get comfortable in my mind.
I want to replenish the trust.
Please see this is a must!

Love Stood with Us

Each day we would search for compassion,
a love that is well groomed and fashioned,
hoping this love would have strong arms
and it would steal our hearts with charms.
As the world continues to be a crazy place,
our new love must be equipped to handle the race.
Even though we might be tired of the run,
we should have the tenacity to endure with fun.

No distance will ever come between.
The mountain will step as side when we are seen.
The troubled world will ask how come
our love stood and now the world must bow.

The confusion will be in a different place,
struggling to understand the joy and love seen in on our faces.
Our hearts will feel satisfied that we have stood the test of time,
and despite all the challenges, we came out with sane minds.

The world will be proud of us.
We have a place with our best friend called trust,
someone who will not let us down.
This energy that can't ever again be destroyed
but will always be around!

Love Delayed Not Denied

I know our love is longer than a scarf
But it feels like I only have half
It felt like the other portion was hidden
And I had to beg for it to be given

As the torment escalated,
I knew everything was being calculated,
hinting to me this delayed would not last
and this setback would pass!

It's just the waiting seems so long.
In the meantime, my heart sang a song.
Patience will bring me what belongs.
Just follow that tiny bread crumb

Urging me not to disturb the moon
The leading sign is planet Neptune.
Not everything is in my control.
Many times, the universe is bold.

It's all a combination to turn one key,
but the main character is me.
In the end, it will all make sense,
and I will understand the suspense!

Love is a Language

Today I finally understood love few languages
It comes in all types of sandwiches
In the early stage, the language can be misunderstood
Like the wolf trying to kill Red Riding Hood!

Test your love today; throw it out in the rain,
shut the door, and long after, check again.
If love is still standing out there,
then that's the only level one, my dear!

Test your love today;
with a trip on the other side of town.
If the heart of love does not frown,
then something is definitely wrong.

Test your love today; tell love it was slack.
If it's real love, it will constantly come back
To protect its owner who is under attack

Test your love today;
just drop love in the middle of nowhere.
If it finds its way back to you,
Then love is not missing any screws.

Love doesn't understand no or leave me alone.
It will only tag the true feeling that it knows
The language of love is true
The languages is extremely few

Unleash Your Love

I had a feeling that you were afraid to love me,
because I felt like you were playing hide and seek!
Why are you afraid of love?
Did someone once take away what was sent from above?

You can trust me to be true.
It's too much work to make you blue.
I know love is waiting locked inside in of you.
Stop caring about people point of views!

Love hid itself whenever I was around.
It kept its face buried in the ground.
When love could not resist any more,
you told me you had to take an immediate tour.

When you left, you took love with you
and gave it a job polishing shoes.
Now love is determined to find its soul,
the place where it can be happy and bold,

The place where it was once secure
and freedom was without limitation and more.
Your love misses my sweet smell and embrace.
Love wants to dry the tears that stream down my face.

Love wants to fix the damage that was done.
I am prepared to work until after the sun goes down
Love knows who is deserving of true love.
And will only make the effort because it must be done!

I Will Not Hurt You

I could tell you were afraid to open up,
so instead you went home and closed your shop.
I screamed till I had no voice.
I screamed some more, giving you a choice.

I really need you more than you know.
Your sweet spirit makes me glow.
Your words are balanced when I'm in doubt.
Our laughter is medicine springing from our mouth!

Your love empowers me to go forward.
I no longer feel like a coward.
I feel strong and brave
since you dragged me out of that cave.

Our sweet energy keeps the fire burning.
This love makes more love; it keeps turning.
Your wisdom fuels; I feel like I am in space.
I am at peace with you when I am face-to-face!

You've touched a special place in my heart.
I often feel a certain spark
telling me that I have found true love
because nothing good in a hurry is coming anytime now

Call my name; I will come running.
I will not turn anything down that's so stunning,
something so unique and beautiful.
This extraordinary woman that fell into my lap

We Belong Together

We belong to each other.
Our relationship is like bread and butter.
We need each other to avoid being dry.
It's good to be on top of each other

You see things that are sometimes no there
Creating extra fuss that doesn't belong to us
Lift your head above the water.
Hold my hand; I will not let us get slaughter.
I only have my love to give.
Release the pass, and then forgive!

The vibration is pounding.
That's love can push down any mountain.
Nothing can stand in the way of love,
because love gets its strength directly from above!

Come sit and have a cup of tea with me.
I will open my heart for you to see.
I will place it in your hands once again.
My love wants to straighten what was bent.

Love doesn't care about what happened yesterday.
Its focus is on how to make things better today.
It will penetrate the problem that hides
and ease the hurt that's dancing about inside.

It does not get any more romantic than this.
How about we take this further than a kiss
Hold my hand and cross over with me.
We have trust, so close your eyes so you can see!

You know we have a future together.
Let's not hide it from one another.
Love does not want to wear any clothes.
Love would rather be completely exposed!

Love Caught Me by the Heart

Love caught me by a hook
when I went to take a look!
I did not plan to be here;
I was just playing in her hair.

When I walked away I was fine,
but I started to feel something inside.
At first I thought it was her sex appeal.
Later my heart unraveled and revealed.

You are in love, young man!
I suggest you adjust and get a plan.
As the fear came to visit me,
telling me to just toss that love in the sea,

I felt an impossible strain.
The love was heavy; I was in pain.
I didn't want to go, to know;
I just wanted to be left alone.

Love knocked on my heart's door,
asking to go to its new lover.
I pretended not to hear.
I think love is talking about the
woman with the sweet-smelling hair.
Did this woman transfer her love disease?
and change my life? It's impossible. Please!
Love doesn't have shape or form.
I think a new love is born.

Just Trust

Please, honey, don't make me wait.
I felt the love; I'm still full of faith.
I want you to come home soon
So it can be us looking at the moon

I know you are trying to make it on your own,
but don't forget to obey the signs as you go along
Listen to that innocent voice inside
Don't be afraid to trust your guide!

We have fought bigger bears.
This one will just give a little scare.
Trust love; it will not let you fall.
It's there if you need anything at all!

Its season's a romantic relationship.
It mends in hard times even wrecked ships.
I have seen love come through for me.
Sweetheart, close your eyes and believe.

Love will keep us nice and warm.
shielding us from a stubborn storm.
Release all fears in the arms of love.
Love will embrace and not shove!

Enough Love

I can hear your heart beat from a mile away,
beating so fast, calling my name.
You wanted a heart-to-heart talk.
Is it is much better than a face-to-face walk?

The heart doesn't need crutches to stand.
Only lies need more than one man.
The truth doesn't need any defense.
Lies will always keep us in suspense.

Face-to-face can sometimes mask the truth.
It might be impossible to get to the root.
Heart–to-heart will always be sure
like when the sun takes its all-day tour!

Heart-to-heart has the magic touch.
It's effortless when you are in love so much.
The answer lies in the deep of the heart.
This will avoid any weeping on our part!

How romantic is this?
Just one touch and we will kiss.
Then we will be one again,
lovers and best of friends!

Let's Settle This First

I can't make love when there are concerns
and my heart complains that it burns.
It's hard for me to go under the sheets
when there are unresolved issues that will not sleep.

I know you think sex would make things right,
but it would just create more friction and fights.
As the problems linger, the love is placed on hold,
the issues need to hurry up and unfold.

Please don't misunderstand me;
but are seeing somebody.
It's just too many late nights on the streets,
and when you come home you never eat.

Your behavior has hinted at a slight change,
but I think it's small enough for us to manage.
I just want to bring it early to the table
so the relationship will not become unstable.

I want you to see the importance of this.
We are the captains of our ships.
If I misunderstood, then tell me so.
I will never think so low.

It bothered me, so I wanted to ask.
Now let's move past and picked up where we were last!

Better Love Life

I know the past couple of years have been rough,
and I know we just about had enough.
Life has been nothing but love tough,
but it's time we focus on just us.

What can we do to improve our love life?
Just something to eliminate the strife
Maybe I can start by letting down my hair,
And try taking unguarded showers with cheer
Our romantic life has been boring.
I know many nights I have been snoring!

I promise today I will get in shape
and have some late-night wine with grapes.
Okay! I will wear something sexy before I come to bed.
I know you would enjoy cherry red!

And I will slow down on watching late-night shows
and come to bed, kissing your toes
I will talk some more when we make love
and remind you that our loves are like hands fit for gloves.

I promise not fall asleep after you smell so sweet.
I will stay awake and play with your feet,
and I promise to use my imagination with you
and put your body in a romantic mood.

How about some red roses spread across the room
and some sweet-smelling perfume?
Some champagne so you can be mine
to pour down your back on time!

Today we vow to not let our relationship get stale
and promise not to put our love life up for sale.
Let's keep the fire burning, always invoking the lust of yearning.
We should always keep the bed protected and warm,
sexy and inviting all year round!

When Our Bodies Call

From all the way across the other side of town,
my body just started tossing around.
When I realized I could not sleep,
I began to think, "What's making me feel so weak?"

In the midst of my silence I could see
all the seductive things you are doing to me.
I felt like I wanted to give a shout,
but right away I had to cover my mouth.

Do you feel the same way on the other side?
Or is it my imagination just gone wild?
No … I feel the same way too.
My mind started to sound like a zoo

Baby, I will not be back for another week.
What can we do so we can fall asleep?
Sometimes when the body calls,
the attention gets demanding and loud.

I'm going to pretend you are right here
and reach for my toys to pretend you are near.
Whatever I see in my vision I will do,
and I will use the appropriate tool.

So even when our bodies are far away,
they call each other without delay.
I get so excited about what I see
using reverse psychology to calm me

I Fell In Love Over the Phone

I fell in love over the phone
I was not sure if I was too old
Something inside told me to take a leap
I just wanted somewhere safe so I can comfortable sleep

Our friends might try to give us an appropriate age
But before they wink we would be engage
So happy no one knows
All we see is each other without any clothes

Smooth sailing in the night
Only one of us likes to fight
Love making, I thought you didn't know
I was surprise you knew those romantic pose

So rewarding the world can't understand
They think it's some kind of secret plan
Because of the world lack of flexibility
It hard for them to see this love ability

I will hold my head high and keep my eyes straight
With this attitude I will bounce off all foolish complaints
They can't beat us, so they will certainly join without fuss
With their faces revealing that love just must!

They don't know what goes on behind closed doors
Judgment and weakness are instantly ignore
Only love in its purist state reside
Rocking with us, falling asleep, after feeling so sweet

No One but Us

No one agreed to this relationship,
so we left and eloped on a ship
alone and safe from the world.
As time lingered, working toward our goal

Life had shown us the path.
Time stood still to give us a head start.
The opportunity came to strengthen us.
This relationship is definitely a must.

Time gave us time to find a sparrow
as life give us multiple arrows.
As the sparrow sang a song,
we knew the steps to follow along.

It only looked confused and doubtful,
but life can sometimes be a handful,
especially when no one agrees.
It could appear less easy.

But what's important is that we have each other
so we can depend and cooperate with one another.
This unknown path that was delivered by mail
everyone is expecting us to fail.

Failure is only when someone refuses a risk.
With one hand, there might be more mistakes.
Two is always better than one; when one is weak,
the other will be strong.

Love Lives

I heard you coming in the wind.
My heart chuckled from within.
I knew you would come for me
after I lifted my head above the sea.

You waited till the storm calmed down,
and when the sun settled beyond,
my heart was torn in two.
I know you felt it too.

Your kisses made me melt inside
those nights when you sang me lullabies,
when you wrapped your arms around me,
covering me so I could not see.

I miss you so much.
I don't care about that stupid fuss.
I know love will keep a meeting with us
and gradually strengthen; it's a must.
Love holds all the correct tools;
love is certainly not a fool.

Love will keep us safe between its wings,
shielding us from the troubles that hide in the wind.
Let's stand up in the name of love.
It will land us safe as we touch the ground.

We can trust love to be the captain of our ship
while we relax comfortably and kiss.
We can turn our backs and leave love to rule.
Love really knows how to keep things cool.

The Impact

Your love impacted my life.
I still cry in fear of the past strife.
I can still see you coming through my front door
with those silly jokes I cheerfully adore!
You always asked the strangest things,
and you could be very detailed about the simplest thing!

I love that funny bone
it tickles me with its mood
You remember how funny you were about those keys?
You kept changing the story; I said, please!

You kept the atmosphere filled with love.
You gave me your new shirt, sent from above.
My heart tells me we will kiss again;
my body yearns to know when.

In the meantime, I will wait and see
if love is as faithful as it promised to be.
I know that life is fair, and
it will not give more than the fair share.
I love you with all my being, and
I look forward to this abundant living ...

Love Soothes Anger

Don't want to waste another day fighting;
the atmosphere becomes uninviting.
Then it's hard to change the moods;
most of the time we have to wait a day or two.

I'm tired of struggling with this.
I've run out of things from my bag of tricks.
I'm out of breadth just to keep up with you.
Sometimes I don't have a clue as to what to do!

We have allowed unwanted factors to get in the way
and cloud our minds of positive things to say.
I'm eager to get our relationship back on track
and stop being so lazy and slack,

To take a chance I might feel pain, but trust I might gain.
Love has the combination to sustain.
Every day is another level of challenging beliefs,
but love will always remain the chief.

If you use love in everything you do,
when you hit rock bottom, it can strengthen too.
Love is an all-rounder;
love is not limited to just one area.

Love can move any mountain,
even the one that presently stands between you and me.
Love can part the roughest path of the seas.
We don't need to ask love please.

Love can cut away strife
into pieces, sharper than a knife.
Love knows how to make perfect love
even if I have my clothes on.

Talk

I would love to communicate
and talk about my mistakes;
show me where I should improve
so my doubts can be removed.

Talking really helps a lot;
it removes all those stubborn blocks.
When a relationship is stuck at sea,
it's those stubborn blocks located beneath.

I would be glad for a dialogue
and not just you talking so loud!
My opinions are important too.
Respect is due regardless of points of view.

How can I make love with a broken heart?
The things you said ripped me apart.
I am so use to being a friend and more,
but it seems like you enjoy going to war.

I just need you to explain to me
what is so hard about saying you're deeply sorry.
In return, I will just shower you with more love,
this unseen gift that traveled from back and beyond.

I am Waiting for Your Love

I gave you the best of me.
I even got on my knees,
expressing the love I believed,
but it was hard for you to receive.

How could you not perceive
My heart! Many late nights; I grieve.
Each time I looked into your eyes,
I was hoping for a sign.

I waited for you to call my name.
Late in the night, I hold the bare flame,
the heat my heart endured.
You must know my love is pure.

Come inside and rest in me.
Let me take the stress away, please!
I will counter fear with my love,
kissing you with tremendous hugs.

My love has become my bodyguard.
It has won every battle with scars.
I am proud in the name of love.
Stand confident with me for love now!

Your Soul Knows

To be with you is so much fun.
I envision us dancing with our first born
All the way till the sun goes down.
We will be making sweet melody
Until we are burnt out

I can never pretend;
I feel the love strong within.
I am eager to obey my soul
in the direction it wants to go.
Even when my mind gets in the way,
my soul fights back to stay sane

My soul insists I should wait
and not be in such a hurry to close my gate.
My soul shows me you feel the same;
It's just a matter of time before you come in!

Your soul cannot deny me,
because we have the same belief.
Even when you ignore your intuition
the soul knows how to petition

Love finds its way somehow.
It understands the principal of how to allow.
Love knows how to fill a cup;
just open your eyes and take a close-up.

Your Love Makes Me Weak

Honey, you are so affectionate.
A gentle touch—I will faint.
A sweet kiss—I don't want to miss it.
A different pose—you must know.

Dripping wet—it must be sweat!
Aggressive man in command
Strong beds—are you there?
Yes! I'm not going anywhere.

Not to worry; I can stand.
I was built for me and my man!
Sweet lips—are you there?
Yes, I'm sitting waiting in my favorite chair.

You can count on me to blow there.
I exist so you don't wear and tear.
Good night time surly flies,
could you delay just for tonight?

I will stand still while you thrill.
Just don't overwork on my grill.
Hello, my love. Circling the room,
I have enough energy for two.
Don't worry; I will play that special drum.
I will make sure to keep the momentum.

Love Will Find a Way

I trust that love will find a way
so you can see beyond your fear.
Love will follow you till you never give up
and will stop you from shopping at the quit shop.

Love will show you how
to make the best of what you have now.
Love will take care of tomorrow
and show you how to work around your sorrows.

Love will find a way
through the challenges that awaits to come in the next day.
Love has a trillion reasons and more
why you should not walk out that door!

Love is confident and thinks only to win.
Love feels how many times you get poked with the same pin.
Love is pure and so divine.
Love's understanding is bigger than your mind.

Love is not afraid to be in a room with fear.
Love will act like fear is not even there!
Love will continue as scheduled
without offending Mr. You-Know–Who.

Love will never second guess.
Love just loves, and its mind is at rest.
Love will sleep in the middle of a storm;
it's impossible for true love to be easily torn!

And if love gets torn,
a new love generation will be born.
Who can destroy love?
Its very existence can't be figured out!
It's so safe to marry love.
It fits perfectly like a glove!

The Love & Faith Test

Today my love was put to the test.
Ever since, my heart has been unrest.
I was so sure I had faith with me
to shield me from the unseen.

I was placed into the fire to get burned.
wondering what I am supposed to learn
I never cursed love or faith;
I was hoping that faith don't make love late

I was thinking that maybe they were late.
To my surprise, I saw them standing at the door,
but I was completely ignored.
I felt like love had left me to die,
and faith watched me while I cried!

As the doubt overwhelmed my soul,
I did not know which way to go.
I thought love and faith were my friends.
I met them both when I was just ten.

They are all I have to depend on.
I'm lost and completely in suspense.
Love was somehow trying to achieve.
Stretching me until I could receive

Faith was pulling every muscle in me,
forcing me to increase my belief.
Love told me it couldn't live with doubt,
and all that needed to be flushed out.

So as they both stretched my heart,
in the process they were cleaning up my path.
I thought I had those two under my belt
but today in my heart I felt—

I felt mad pain, but I remain sane.
I woke up singing in the rain.
Love and faith never left my side,
even in the times when I cried.

The test was to make me strong
and make room for more rewards.
I will give love and faith a big kiss.
never forgetting the fiery test.

I Need to See You

I never thought I would feel like this.
After that night when we kissed,
I was not sure, but I felt something instantly.
From that point on it was constantly.

The feeling follows me wherever I go,
even in my silence on my way home.
I can't believe this is happening to me.
I long to see you for a relief!

I was shy to let you know
how I felt, so I kept it low!
Sometimes I think you feel the same,
but you look for something else to blame.

I would love to see you again
to confirm these feelings,
but I don't know when!
It feels like it could be anytime soon.
All I know is it will be before the full moon.
If this is a dream, please come and see me.

Tell me that you don't feel
because your heart seems to be made of steel.
Convince me that I'm not the one
and I will be gone!

Let Me Love You

Please come into the bedroom.
Let's not break any rules.
Love brought us safe and sound
from the crazy world under the ground.

Real romance is on our side.
Honey, just put away your pride.
You can start slowly with a kiss.
I know it's hard for you to do this.

Mistakes are there to make.
Once we can recognize and learn from it,
there is no need for us to wait.
Lets romance like there is no tomorrow

Some problems are unacceptable,
others are manageable,
but ours are definitely fixable.

Let's seize the moment.
There is so much room for improvement,
but it's hard to achieve this without any movement.

Lay your head on my chest;
rest comfortably between my breasts.
Look at me from a different point of view
and pack up all those crazy blues!

Where Are You

Where are you? My heart jumped!
My soul immediately got all dressed up.
Love told me, you were stopping by.
Three of us cannot be denied.

I know love would not lie,
but I figure you had a freckled mind.
When I saw night fall,
I thought at least you would call.

Darling, just follow your soul.
It knows where to go.
My love has been faithful and strong.
Come while the night is still young.

Are you afraid of the love that dwells in me?
Love told me not to worry,
you would come around and believe.
Tomorrow a new day is born.
Listen to your heart blow its horn.

Make Love to Me

I don't want to spend another empty night.
Come under the sheets; it will feel right!
Pour some oil; rub my shoulders.
Run your fingers over my twin towers.

Come into my palace,
where you will find no malice.
Squeeze my heart tight
till my soul turns on its light.

Cause me to dance with the moon and stars.
Let your touch remove those stubborn bars.
Right now in this moment,
I will not let my pride give any comment.

You feel good in my arms.
I'm happy we gave our love a chance.
It's worth fighting for.
I'm so thrilled we brought our relationship to shore.

I will never take us for granted.
Our love is implanted
in the depths where it can't be lost,
safe just for us!

When I saw you at the front door,
my heart gladly dropped to the floor.
When I heard you say my name,
I knew no one was to be blamed.

I wanted to know how long you planned to stay.
You told me once, never stand in the way."
I've been waiting for such a long time.
I was starting to think time was not on my side.

You really made me sweat.
For months I sat and fret
Make love to me while I stand.
I'm confident this will go as I planned.

I Love You a Million

When I met you, my life was dancing in heat!
I did not even have a spoon to eat!
Mentally, I was trying to stay sane,
but with patience I was hoping to gain.
When I first met you, I was not sure;
I thought you wanted to get laid and nothing more!

After you saw the struggles in my eyes,
You said, "We can improvise!"
I was moved with compassion
as my heart left the floor,
thinking you are the man I consciously adore!

Since then I am always thinking of how to appear.
You always said you look great my dear!
I dreamt of entertaining you in a special way,
something for you to remember at work all day!

Let go into our bedroom and talk some more
Let's wrestling until we hit the floor!
Let's fight until we both get soaking wet!
Rumbling and tumbling all over in each other's sweat!
Pulling my hair with all your might,
putting more fiction in the fight!

I don't want this pleasure to end;
let's freeze time and pretend!
I really do not want this tussle to end.
I don't want morning to come for me and say,
The end!

To the Good Life

Cheers to the good life.
I have successfully eliminated all strife!
Today I am sure it's tough luck
for the one who feels insecure.

I feel no pain, only
the smooth energy that I've gained!
I have no regrets, because life never forgets.

I don't feel alone,
because love has placed me on top of the world.
I have not lost anything.
Confirmation feels like a tingling!

Today I will not rush,
because whoever is outside would be crushed.
Safe sensation has filled my space.
That special face will finds its place.

I will turn the tables around,
and this time you will frown.
Right now I have the control.
I am opening the door for you to stroll.

Hands down, head bowed,
telling me you didn't understand how.
Gently kiss, telling me you miss this.

Sorry; you wish you were not in a hurry.
So late you are fighting to open my gate!

When Love Feels

Love was looking for a simple confession
Just to start a new session.
Deception causes depression.
If not careful, the relationship
will go unto a state of regression!

Love will not willfully transgress.
It's sole purpose is to progress.
Lies will not find its way to success.
If there is no truth, love will never get dress.

If love is in distress
It will struggle, to impress.
If love feels disappointed
It will still attempt to climb any mountains.

It's hard for love to fully rest.
As the days go by, it's exposed to less.
Love will forgive a million times.
It doesn't even cost a dime.

Love will take a risk and stay,
hoping you will open up and say,
expressing your truth that resides,
that you no longer want to hide.

Love Has No Gender

Have you heard of someone called love?
This energy can fill any void.
The cares of the world imprisoned you?
Love is here, armed to rescue.

Love has no gender
Genuine love will freely surrender.
Love don't care about color
It will only move on if rejected for another

To feel love in its purest state,
you have to be open, to escalate
without being afraid of height.
There is no room for might.

Love dwells where it's wanted
and hides when its feels frustrated and hunted
When love is happy; all the way, love says
this trip must not be delayed.
Safe and sound, love is around
Smile and receive your love crown

Love Will Stand Up

How bad do you want me?
I know we must disagree to agree.
I'm not going to cry one more time.
I did not commit any crime.

I'm doing the best for us to make it.
We have one more chance to change things.
Baby, let's hold on to each other
and fight for one another.

We came into this to be together forever.
Let's trust love in this bad weather.
I've been standing up, trusting love.
The problem is not just going to magically get solved.

I have enough faith for you and me,
but just give a helping hand along with your belief
If I'm wrong, then you can be gone.
I will take off before the sun plays its favorite song

Are you afraid to know what you might feel?
I think you know it will be real.
Near or far, love will not be hidden.
This magical feeling was divinely given.

Our love did not drop from the sky,
as much as you try to deny.
Safely our love was born;
quietly it was torn.

I have searched the highs and lows
for a sign to let me know
if it's okay to find a place to go.
I would leave town and search for love in the snow.

I know my place is with you.
It seems impossible that it will come through,
but love assure once before me it knows what to do.
Love can tie its own shoe,

So today I will not trust what I see
and swim with my heart in the depths of the sea
where all the danger lies in wait,
guarding the love's gate!

Love holds a special key
that will no doubt release me,
a key that danger cannot comprehend,
and on that day you will not pretend.

As the sun went down to rest,
my heart took the time to get dressed.
I turned around to see if you were really gone.
I heard you whispering a sweet hello song,
promising you would be back today
to renew your love that you took away.

Love Knows When

Love never dies; it feels pain when I cry.
Crying doesn't mean that it's over;
you might just need a shoulder.
All is not lost, my dear.
Don't wonder with fear.

Trust faith with all your heart,
knowing you will find him on your path.
I know it looks like when,
but don't let time build a fence.

Don't allow time to entrap you.
It's okay if today you feel blue.
Your spirit was just short of some roots,

Trust love for you to see
even with the nails sticking in your feet.
Life will not let you down,
even when trouble is circling around.

The love paths are sometimes hard to wear
But love faithfully stays near
Love will get you there when you should;
don't worry about whether life could.

I know you feel like life is passing by,
watching you like a helpless child.
Life loves you more than you;
your dreams are just about to come true!

Love Can Be Rough

I bought our favorite bottle of rum.
I was expecting you to come
There's no escape; I'm dying to see your sexy shape.

Smooth talking, rough playing.
Tonight there will be some obeying.
You will be submissive to all my needs.
I will not be saying please!

You are the woman I love.
Allow me to put on those handcuffs.
Kissing and loving; there's no need for convincing.
Bed squeaking, we are playing.
No one is disturbing.

I'm so happy to be close to you.
Our relationship feels brand new.
The struggle made me sweat.
I've never been bored with you yet!

Passion

I heard passion say,
I am here forevermore;
once you unlock your door,
I will never judge or get upset.
I am here! "Get ready" Set!

I see the hurt in your soul
All crushed up; silently complaining of the cold
Let's enter a new phase with grace;
Let me put a clean sexy smile on your face.

If you just open the door a little more,
your heart will be picked up off the floor.
Trust the feelings that reside within;
answer the questions that's sticking you with that pin.

You held on for dear life;
you spoke words that shed light.
Place your head in the comfort of me.
Listen to your heart saying: believe, believe.

Let Love Awaken You

Let me wake those shoulders that are sound asleep;
let me rub those other members that continuously squeak.
I see the constant drama that runs down your face;
You long for someone genuine to embrace.

Give me another chance to compromise
I will bend backwards with a nice surprise
I will do anything to keep our soul alive
I will try not to fight the inevitable
And welcome the unthinkable

Let love shine its light to reveal
into our bedroom to be heal
I will give love the keys to come in,
making sure darkness has no invitation again.

I know fear has put you to the test,
Standing on top of your chest
Even when you run and hide
Love understands when you act like a child.

Let love awaken my prince charming
I can't wait for you to open your eyes my darling!
You have been asleep for too long
I know loving you was never wrong

Let love lead you to the shore;
From the exhausted waters that kept you a whore
Love will purify and keep us dignify

So Much Love for You

Tonight I placed my hands on my chin,
wondering where you might have been.
I drunk a warm cup tea under the canopy,
thinking, when are you going to come back home to me?

As I lay on the other side,
I long for you to come inside.
Winds blow; energy flows.
I would love to kiss you at least on your nose.

I miss your touch that made me safe;
I try to imagine your embrace
I am in love with you
and more since you have gone.
My heart is walking around with a frown.

I am worried that you may not feel the same,
but my heart confirms that we are on the same page.
How many nights I've cried myself to sleep
wondering if you would surprise between the sheets.

It's hard for me to trust another man.
I'd rather go create a crime.
I am not going to look for replacement for your shoe;
I am in love with only you.
I keep asking myself why the time apart;
I am unable to understand my heart.
I mended our relationship with a substance stronger than glue
each time I made love to you.

My heart keeps telling me not to move,
but I feel like my heart every day is being bruised.
Just so you know, I love you so,
a river that will continue to flow!

A New Love Is Born

In the morning when I saw the rose,
it felt like I had no clothes,
I know then I came out again from my mother's womb?
A place where there were no rules?
Somewhere where I once hide?
I knew I was born to someday die.

No questions stood in the way;
nobody told me I had to pay.
No doubt painted my walls.
Stress was definitely unable to call.

Sweet fruits hung from the tree.
Honey sprung out automatically.
The bread was abundant; all mine.
I was a happy woman inside.

I enjoyed feeding from that tube.
I never encountered the blues.
From the inside, I heard all the pain,
all the screaming and crying; surely it wasn't in vain.

Where Is My Love

As I lay in the darkest of the day,
I was tired from the mental run.
I asked the guard anxiously, "Where is the one?"
He said, "Over the hill till the sun goes down!"

I did not know shape or form,
only the journey that was almost done!
I could not see who it was,
only a feeling that my life had just begun.

My heart said love is at the door.
I arose to check; feeling unsure!

My heart applauded with a loud
voice as time stood still so I could stare.
Truly my burdens had instantly disappeared!

I could not believe what I had just seen!
It was worth the mental tour.
No time to stop and think if it's for sure;
I am in love, and I believe that there is more.

Making Love

I am going to do my best to impress him
and brighten up what looks grim
with my soda-bottle shape.
One look at me, and he wouldn't want to wait.

Baby gave me that seductive kiss
Wait for my permission to remove your lips
Can you wear your favorite cologne?
The one you use so I don't answer the phone

Make love to me with that sexy underwear
Don't worry I know how to tear
No limitation; you have my permission
The atmosphere is in perfect condition

Honey, break down my heart that's filled with
doubt. Make love to me with that ferocious mouth!
Sink in your claw until it pierces my soul.
Sink deeper till you will find the second door

Make room for real love to flow.
Allow our sweet sensation to begin to grow.
Let our love making intensify
Doing our best to modify

Run those curious fingers down there
brushing your tongue to remove my hair
Grip my waistline as I buckle up real tight
I know I can handle this rough flight

Just Believe

I've been trying to forget,
but my heart will not regret.
My main concern is to be sure
and hope my heart doesn't ignore.

The times we spent are sealed
I know the universe will reveal
I don't want my soul to get stuck
or my heart to be mocked.

Some lights, please!
The universe said no; believe!
Can't see where I'm going;
I feel like I'm floating.

Some hugs and kisses, please!
Patience; love is bringing the keys—
the one key that will unlock
the treasure of his soul that was blocked.

These special keys lie within.
Do nothing; just stick a pin.
Even when you are in doubt,
Just believe, while you zip your mouth

so you can't turn the key,
Just leave it be!
Don't give up hope.
Love is able to help you cope!

You Will Love

You told me you didn't love me,
but in my heart I'm still going to believe.
You admit you cannot feel;
I will patiently wait for your heart to reveal

Pretty soon, I will be all yours.
It will be so simple just because
you are not invincible,
yet you have caused so much love trouble.

Not to worry—patience knocked at my door,
It reminded that you are a chore!
It's clear you have convinced yourself
That you are going to remain with dust on the shelf.

My heart told me if I played my cards right
you would willingly walk back into my life.
I have some tricks up my sleeves.
I'm not going to be the good girl you perceive

Same approach, same result
My love life will continue to be an insult
Different approach, different result
My love life will never need to consult….

Follow the Next Step

Follow the next step
Even if you risk the chance of getting wet
Fewer questions and things will unfold.
Answers will never get old

Some answers don't have a plan!
It is guarantee to show up without a helping hand.
Everything takes care because life never sleeps
Let love calm your nerves
and walk with you around those troubled curves.

The person who broke your heart in two
will definitely spend many nights about you.
Difficulty will always stand in his way
until he turns around and says

It was me from day one
creating trouble along with fun!
Confused, mixing the two,
walking around to abuse!

I'm the only one who believes love will return.
My soul longs and yearns.
Maybe I will risk getting burned,
but my heart told me not to be concerned.

My chances are up in the air.
There is no room for fear.
Today I will gamble on love,
because in my mind, it was sent in its purest state from above.

Love Will Return

Love told me to wait at the gate,
to stand firm, to just have some faith.
It promised me it would be back to finish our trips.
I'm worried; I think I'm losing my grip!

Love left a long time ago.
This process is moving too slow.
Impatient, I can't wait,
so faith will have to wait.

I will follow the tracks of love
or just start walking around,
calling love aloud.
Why did love temporarily leave?
Maybe just for a little relief

Love promised to stay.
What could have caused this delay?
I can't wait for a new day to be born,
to mend what was torn.

I'm Confident about Love

I knew you could not do without my love.
I'm unique—sealed, signed, and sent from the divine
There is no love like this.
It was scary, but I followed the bliss.

I feel more confident about love each day
It grows every time I recognize my name
This morning, when I rise,
I spoke to the universe before I opened my eyes.
I thanked it for the new day
and the opportunity for things to flow my way.

As I segmented my morning,
I spoke the words affirmation.
I looked for the bliss;
I embrace love with a thank you kiss.

No questions asked, I just performed the task.
Sure enough, I was confident
There was never a day that love showed me any resentment

You Finally Came

In the midnight hour, you came to me.
Oh, what a sign of relief!
I was almost out of breath.
My heart would daily fret.

When you came I felt the freedom
You relieved me from serpent's venom
I had regain my confidence
Your love came and removed the fence

Undress me now with your intelligence,
come closer; I'm smelling your favorite fragrance,
Many nights I left the lights on in my heart
So when you come in it would not a problem to start

Allow my finger tips to poke your nose,
I want to be sure you were the person that left without clothes
As I closed my eyes to see,
You caused the stars to come down and sit with me.

I don't want to say good night just yet.
It feels like this is the first time I am having sex.
it feels right being nude,
I'm enjoying; as I lost myself in this overwhelming mood.

My body will stay in constant devotion
Making love in slow motion
Reaching places higher than the sky
Removing all limitation that once reside

You Will Commit

My heart told me that you would commit
despite your reluctances to admit
I figured out what would make you submit.
I will wait patiently till life permits.

Nothing can happen without first a thought.
You didn't commit because your heart fought.
Sex alone cannot turn the key;
I need to know that your love is real.

I have traveled a long way from home
across the desert in that terrible storm.
You will commit after this long chase;
I plan on winning this race.

Resist all you want; you don't have to agree
I will not allow you to just leave me
I'm the best you ever had;
with all the wrong you did, I never stayed mad.

I will stand with open arms when you come with cheer.
as your heart receives me standing there
In that moment time will set the stage.
One wink and we will be on the same page.

The love doesn't get any better than this.
If the world comes in my way, I will show my fist.
I will fight with every drop of blood for a commitment
Even if in the end we end up resent!

Let's Talk

I want to come home to a place free to roam,
where my speech is not criticized, and where my actions are left alone!
I'm not looking for someone to put me on the witness stand,
but I want a strong person to become my right hand!

Sometimes I feel like I'm in the lion's den,
receiving scratching all over my head.
If I can't come to you, where should I go?
On the street corner where the girls say hello?

I want to come home and share my concerns with you.
I wish you would have an open mind; because we are two.
A man's house should be his resting spot
with his lady dancing and cooking on a hot pot!

I see you when your eyes are closed
the guilt shining through your nose
You have kept me in suspense so often about you,
but through these lenses, I can see your trend.

I will not let anything get in the way of us.
We just have to make sure and guard our trust.
Sometimes I feel I need a special friend,
someone who is honest and will not pretend.

You often threaten to walk out before drawn.
Many nights I've heard movements on the lawn.
I just trust and go back to sleep as I yawn.
Thanking god that nothing will be torn

I Love You The Most

Out of everyone, I love you the most.
Why are you so afraid to leave your post?
Trust me I will take care you there
Use baby steps; it will bring you near

I normally don't do second rounds,
but love has placed my feet on solid ground.
Backward can be a good step; forward I
don't know what's going to happen next.

Surely this must be a sign
to pay attention to what could possibly be mine.
Yesterday your hands felt cold.
Then love told me you have trouble being bold.

Give me your heart, and I will lead.
I will stop the hurt that's making you bleed
Please, baby, trust me.
Just love me under those sheets.

I love you the most.
I'm not a ghost.
Baby, it's okay to leave your post.

I could not wait to see your face.
I wanted us to stand in the same place.
I've missed your tender kisses so long.

I know we belonged.

I know you felt the heated passion,
as you fought to keep old fashioned.
How do I make you see?
our love is inevitable; it must be.

You can climb the highest mountain;
And still never find a genuine love fountain.
I'm the best lover in the land;
I can please any man.You Promise

Promises are a comfort for a fool
I would rather not be used as a toy tool
I committed without a ring
Hoping to hear your best man would sing

How long would it take you to say: I do"
I 'm sure quicker than you can say: I Love You"
I'm dying to hear the bells say:
A least you finally made it here"

I only have eyes for you,
and when I change my clothes,
all I think about is pleasing you.

When I first met you,
I decided it would last.
I said let our past be the past

Take my hand and come inside.
Feel the fire that burns as my heart cries
Hold on tight and don't let go;
Let's not make false promises and our love a puppet show

The Love That Flows

Every now and then I stop and stare,
wondering how I arrived here!
I remembered when you just disappeared.
My heart was overwhelmed with fear.

I used my love to bring you back
and give your mistakes a good whack!
I doubted every time a negative thought intervenes;
As it 'got so hard for me to believe the unseen.

I saw us kissing romantically in your eyes.
To be with you was always a delight.
I can't imagine going through life and old
without having the opportunity to bear you a soul!

It's not just your body that's attractive.
It's the degree of your heavy love making—so addictive.
I enjoy the love that flows.
My hearts laughs and glows.

Your annoyance exceeds where I stand.
I will keep my peace and treat you like a man.
Your protection brought me safe to shore.
Your tenderness was too hard to ignore.

Your romance was filled with so much certainty,
causing a flood of love to overwhelm me.
Every day you showered me with your romance
in the bathroom where we nakedly danced!

will never dance with another fish!
You alone have kept my interest.
It's not about how many fishes
swim in the deep;
it's about the foundation you
laid before me, so neat!

What's Keeping Us Apart

Is it me that's keeping us apart?
If so, why didn't you say so from the very the start?
You seemed happy and comfortable; it's been a year!
Our relationship was never in trouble with tears

Is it the make-up on my face?
You told me that my smile lighten the place.
Is it the quality of my hair?
You said it matched perfectly with my black lingerie.

You always complimented me on my jokes
You didn't care who would look
I lost some weight as you indirectly suggested!
Why the relationship seems more infested?

What faults are harming our relationship?
What's keeping us apart, causing you to skip?
Tell me again; what you would like me to do?
Let's regroup before you say we are through.

I cried many nights when I didn't understand
why you up and left, abandoning our labored plan.
You left me alone picking up the pieces on the floor!
And your actions did not line up anymore!

I'll be here as long as life permits,
but remember you were the one that split!
When we met, I was dying to commit.
Now it feels like I'm holding
the shitty end of the stick!

Embrace this preciousness that was given for free.
You did not labor; you weren't asked for an entrance fee.
Life trusted you with a heart filled with beauty,
but you walked out on your line of duty!

Hot and cold, I tried to know,
but your behavior was extremely bold.
Come back before time closes the gate.
Not even faith will help you if you are late!

I loved you without thinking twice.
I would never trade you for mice.
I will meet you at the same place.
I hope I meet you on that day,
I will gladly embrace!

Pain with Love

Pain came wrapped up in a bunch,
disguised; I mistakenly had it for lunch.
Even when my stomach ached, I continued to munch.
Covered with beauty, bitter mixed with sweet,
it tasted so good, I continued to eat!

As the bad feeling circled inside,
believe me! The pain was so bad; I wanted to die.
At first, I could not sort it out.
thinking it was love that took me down a painful route.

To my surprise, I began to feel
the hurt came along disguised with love to eat.
As I retraced my steps to see,
There it the pain was hidden beneath.

I was stunned to learn what I did not want to see,
a beast creating fake love in the deep,
fixing sandwiches just for me to eat.
My heart cried without passion.
It had contaminated the sea.

I was so wide awake I could not see
what he was doing to me.
I had set this trap for myself,
The minute I felt that familiar snap!

At the depths of the ocean, I have seen
all the ruthless things being done to me.
I feel like a soldier called for war,
but good thing I am always ready for more!

Give Him Space

If you love him, then let him go;
stepping aside will allow him to grow!
Honor the space that's due to him,
and allow life to give him a mature trim.

Planning love; maybe he has many doubts!
Just be confident with a quiet mouth
As you silence your heart; avoiding a shout!

If you force you might find
something that might make you
shift before the right time;
it might be too strong for your nose,
and quitting may not be the immediate way to go!

Trust is the most powerful tool.
Use it; it will not break any rules.
Everyone deserves some time to retreat.
Doing each other a favor and
staying a few feet!

We both have fundamental rights;
let's respect each other without fights.
Don't assume and try to intervene.
You need confidence to be a man's queen.

If there is someone else,
his behavior will let you know.
Men ran a high risk, giving all their trust,
He will not retreat because he is disgust!

If there is something pressing on your heart,
use soft words to impart.
I often give you your space.
Please don't put a frown on my face.

Release my throat, and don't hold my nose.
Otherwise I can't smell your precious rose.
I have no secrets hidden from you.
I would not go through the trouble to be untrue!
It's better to live a life of reality
than a life of fantasy

Let's Start Again

I don't want to make love upset
I feel like you have not heard my side of the story yet
Please give me a chance to state my truth
Why does it always have to be about you?

I probably when overboard with a loud voice
And because of this you threw me under the bus
Sometimes I am not good at expressing clearly
Don't use this opportunity to take advantage of me!

I may not be clear about a lot of things
but I am clear about my never-ending love that resides within
I wear my love for you and the world to see
but you always find a fault and use it to challenge me

And then when I open my mouth to say:
You somehow find your hands in my underwear
Making love is for two who cannot resist
Not to polish and fix our mistakes

Reasoning to agree and disagree
Will put our hearts to rest and be at ease
Communication is not for fool
Please do not use sex as a quick fix-it tool!

Please Believe In Me

What must I do to convinced you
I ended all limitation just win you
Your silence makes me nervous
My hearts going into a stage of unconscious

I didn't have to let you know
Could of look at you through my window
I could have pretend; you would of never knowing when

Don't allow your heart be deceive
Look into my eyes and perceive
Check to see if my words line up with my action
and how you feel when I extend my affection

A relationship is build on trust
If we don't have this, it will quickly turn into dust
I desire something real
An atmosphere where I am free to reveal

All the things that make me feel afraid
Don't want to hold in it to make our relationship fade
Let's dance in truth and love
because all we have is us
Safe and sound you will be; always with me!

Late-Night Shower

I love taking late-nights showers
As I take my time to exercise my powers
with my legs wrapped around you, with a kiss—
it's been so long; I truly miss

Hold my waist firm and tight;
press toward me hard tonight.
Run your fingers through my hair;
rub down my invisible underwear.

Pick me up with your strength so strong!
I will use my legs to anchor; just spine me around.
Kiss me as my heart begins to race.
Hold my tongue; firmly in its place!

Allow the water to beat on my face.
Shut your eyes; as I happily taste.
your inside feel so warm and sweet!
I love when you take me down Love Street!

Gently lure my head back, as you kiss my neck,
I am so excited, and we haven't had sex yet!
I enjoy surrendering my body to you.
I know you will meet every need like you always do!

Don't hold out on me; I am able to stand.
I will adjust to whatever you have planned!
In the shower we will be
Enjoying late night showers,
just you loving me!

Thinking Deeper

Relationships can have some tedious work
Being single allows appreciation; realizing worth
Two conflicting-agreeable personalities
Truthfully no one is ever please!

You can be in a relationship and be so alone
and single feeling extremely whole
looking for someone to compliment me
and not lazy taking up space in my sheets

I am finally satisfied with myself
That trying to many lovers made little sense
I thought I lack secure; was hoping
people would help me achieve more!

Safe and sound it was a rough ride
but with little or no confidence I manage not to die
learning to take one step at a time
and stop second guessing the divine

Let's exchange numbers
In denial that the universe had uncover
Missing the point completely
Maybe this was not to be forever with me
People come for a season reason and lifetime
I have accepted and when the time comes I am ready to say goodbye!

About the Author

In love too many times
giving my genuine love to the swine's
Quality is so difficult to find
and quantity was always naked standing by.

So exhausted from not skipping any steps
The lesson was harshly taught; only when
I started loving myself!

So happy the universe kept its word
and patiently waited for me to come home
Many nights I thought it was my last chance
Then the universe whispered;
Stop being so swift to take off your pants!

I thought if I give all the love I had
I would spend the rest of my life in "ferry" land
Life taught me not to give my love for free
because quality and respect doesn't grow on trees

Genuine love can be abused and misused
The experience kept me isolated and confused
but life kept my head above the water
and my strong will prohibited me from going under!

Life is fair game
and the good news is I have no shame!
I've lost many love battles
but I had enough guts to always tackle another
with the new information saturated in my mind
I have stop being unworthy for the last time!